Understanding Cosmetic Procedures:
Surgical and Nonsurgical

Efrain Arroyave, MD
In association with Aestheticus.org

THOMSON

DELMAR LEARNING™

Australia • Brazil • Canada • Mexico • Singapore • Spain • United Kingdom • United States

THOMSON
DELMAR LEARNING

Understanding Cosmetic Procedures:
Surgical and Nonsurgical
Efrain Arroyave, MD

President, Milady:
Dawn Gerrain

Director of Editorial:
Sherry Gomoll

Acquisitions Editor:
Brad Hanson

Editorial Assistant:
Jessica Burns

Director of Production:
Wendy A. Troeger

Production Editor:
Nina Tucciarelli

Production Assistant:
Angela Iula

Composition:
Graphic World Inc.

Director of Marketing:
Wendy Mapstone

Channel Manager:
Sandra Bruce

Marketing Coordinator:
Nicole Riggi

Cover Design:
Joseph Villanova

COPYRIGHT © 2006 Thomson Delmar Learning, a division of Thomson Learning, Inc. Thomson Learning™ is a trademark used herein under license.

Printed in the United States of America
1 2 3 4 5 XXX 09 08 07 06 05

For more information, contact Delmar Learning, 5 Maxwell Drive, Clifton Park, NY 12065-2919
at http://www.milady.com and www.thomsonlearning.com

ALL RIGHTS RESERVED. No part of this work covered by the copyright hereon may be reproduced or used in any form or by any means—graphic, electronic, or mechanical, including photocopying, recording, taping, Web distribution or information storage and retrieval systems—without the written permission of the publisher.

For permission to use material from this text or product contact us by
Tel (800) 730-2214
Fax (800) 730-2215
www.thomsonrights.com

Library of Congress Cataloging-in-Publication Data

Arroyave, Efrain.
  Understanding cosmetic procedures: surgical and nonsurgical / Efrain Arroyave, in association with Aestheticus.org.
      p. ; cm.
  Includes bibliographical references and index.
  ISBN 1-4018-9745-2 (softbound)
  ISBN 978-1-4018-9745-1
1. Surgery, Plastic. 2. Skin—Surgery. 3. Skin—Care and hygiene.
  [DNLM: 1. Cosmetic Techniques. 2. Reconstructive Surgical Procedures. 3. Skin Care. WO 600 A779u 2006]
  I. Aestheticus.org. II. Title.

RD119.A767 2006
617.9″5—dc22

2005026620

NOTICE TO THE READER

Publisher does not warrant or guarantee any of the products described herein or perform any independent analysis in connection with any of the product information contained herein. Publisher does not assume, and expressly disclaims, any obligation to obtain and include information other than that provided to it by the manufacturer.

The reader is expressly warned to consider and adopt all safety precautions that might be indicated by the activities herein and to avoid all potential hazards. By following the instructions contained herein, the reader willingly assumes all risks in connection with such instructions.

The publisher makes no representation or warranties of any kind, including but not limited to, the warranties of fitness for particular purpose or merchantability, nor are any such representations implied with respect to the material set forth herein, and the publisher takes no responsibility with respect to such material. The publisher shall not be liable for any special, consequential, or exemplary damages resulting, in whole or part, from the readers' use of, or reliance upon, this material.

This book is **dedicated** to my wife, Robin; my children, Cali Victoria and Aaron Joseph; and our dear friends, Larry, Debra, and Clint Chilson, for their encouragement and support.

Efrain Arroyave, MD

Contents

SECTION FOUR

SECTION FIVE

Foreword

I am privileged to write this foreword.

Dr. Arroyave knows how strongly I feel about education in aesthetic medicine. A vital part of my career has been in disseminating information about new approaches, advances, and successes with medical colleagues, ancillary team players, and the general public.

In the past decade, cosmetic surgery has entered a new age. Advances, technical refinements, and a vast assortment of product lines have enabled hundreds of thousands of people throughout the world to experience changes in their appearance, and consequently, their lives.

Although plastic and reconstructive surgeons, facial plastic surgeons (otolaryngologists), and dermatologists are at the core of this metamorphosis, the medical team has now expanded to include a large number of paraprofessionals, including estheticians, who help prepare the patient's skin for these procedures, and who care for their skin afterward. This well-written text by Dr. Arroyave, and the impressive group of physicians who contributed their expertise, is written specifically for them. Yet, the average person can read and understand it as well.

The content of this book is thorough and easy to read and comprehend. This book will enable esthetician and massage therapy schools around the world to maximize the understanding of common cosmetic procedures in the training process of their students. In addition, this book is destined to be a continual resource for the thousands of skin care specialists now being hired by dermatologists and plastic surgeons who provide preoperation preparation and postoperation care or state-of-the-art treatments in the office.

Understanding Cosmetic Procedures is one of the first textbooks of its kind for this group of paraprofessionals. I wish them well in their careers.

Lawrence B. Robbins, MD, FACS
President and Chairman of the Board of Trustees
The American Society of Aesthetic Plastic Surgery, 1997–1999;
Clinical Associate Professor of Plastic and Reconstructive Surgery
University of Miami School of Medicine

Preface

Today **aesthetic medical practitioners** have a myriad of treatment modalities and surgical procedures to fool the hands of time. Along with these medical-surgical advances in aesthetics, advanced scientific formulations for topical skin care products and oral nutritional supplements for the skin are entering this multibillion-dollar beauty industry at a rapid pace.

Cosmetic surgery and *aesthetic surgery* are synonymous terms.

WHY THIS BOOK IS NOW ESSENTIAL

To better deal with the public's demand for *comprehensive skin care,* most busy aesthetic medical practitioners are hiring skin care specialists to work with their patients for preprocedure and postprocedure (and maintenance) skin care. Most of these skin care specialists come from the ranks of estheticians; others are nurses, medical assistants, and physicians' assistants.

Yet, even as we witness an increase in advanced skin care training programs across the country, there is a lack of textbooks on the medical-surgical side of aesthetics for those skin care specialists who endeavor to better understand the medical-surgical perspective of the most popular aesthetic medical procedures available today.

This book prepares skin care specialists with a better understanding of the rationale, selection, timing, and application of skin care regimens as they pertain to their clients facing any form of surgical or nonsurgical aesthetic procedure. This well-organized, easily understood, systematic approach to the medical side of aesthetics can be used as a textbook for the student or as a reference book for the practicing skin care specialist.

WHAT THIS BOOK PROVIDES

Understanding Cosmetic Procedures is divided into surgical and nonsurgical sections. Although frequently used interchangeably, surgery is a procedure, but a procedure is not necessarily surgery (e.g., a chemical face peel is a procedure but is not surgery). Another way to differentiate the two is by using the terms *invasive* and *noninvasive* procedures. In general, if a **scalpel** is used to penetrate the dermis the procedure is more likely to be surgical (invasive). For our purposes, the term *procedure* will be used interchangeably for both surgical and nonsurgical applications.

Our exclusive intent is to give the reader a better understanding of the most common and popular aesthetic methods available today, as well as exposure to an array of alternative and ancillary procedures. The photos and graphics are not intended to impress but rather to enable the reader in understanding a particular procedure.

Throughout the text, numerous *medical terms* are bolded and either immediately defined or defined in the glossary. Each chapter is broken down into topics pertinent to specific aesthetic procedures, including:

- Indications
- Mechanisms of action and target tissues
- Preprocedure considerations, including anesthesia
- General procedure techniques
- Dressings and wound care, including sutures, bathing, hair care, makeup, and sun protection
- Postprocedure skin/tissue changes, including scarring
- Postprocedure activities
- Risks and possible complications

This is not a "how-to" manual. **Contraindications** for procedures are not discussed, as they are outside the scope of this book. It is assumed that the reader has a *basic* understanding of the anatomy and physiology of the skin. Further, because the science presented here is general medical information found in any number of plastic surgery and dermatology books, no particular references are cited. However, for the section on oral antioxidants, a reference list is provided.

AESTHETIC MEDICAL EDUCATIONAL RESOURCES, INC.

DBA: Aestheticus.org

Founded in 2001 by an esthetician, a registered pharmacist, a nurse-esthetician, a nurse-pharmaceutical representative, and a physician's assistant, this not-for-profit organization facilitates continuing education courses in **aesthetic medicine** to nonphysician healthcare professionals and estheticians who endeavor to better understand the medical-surgical side of aesthetic medicine.

Aestheticus.org is independent of but works with hospitals, medical societies, medical academies, and busy aesthetic medicine practitioners to design and present continuing education (CE) courses around the United States. These CE courses are designed for accreditation by pertinent regulatory boards and/or respective governing bodies.

In 2003, *Aestheticus.org* produced a 12-part cable TV series on *Advances in Spa Skin Care* with board-certified dermatologists, plastic and reconstructive surgeons, and facial plastic surgeons (otolaryngologists), as well as spa directors from the Ritz Carlton, the Mandarin Hotel, and Turnberry Isle Spa and Resort in South Florida.

In 2004, *Aestheticus.org* launched a pilot externship program for estheticians, medical assistants, nurses, and other qualified skin care specialists to spend 70 hours observing busy **aesthetic medical practitioners.** The pilot program was a success and is expanding nationally. For more information on this externship program visit http://www.Aestheticus.org.

In 2003, Milady challenged *Aestheticus.org* to produce this book to meet the needs of a growing population of skin care specialists in today's vital aesthetic medical practices. In turn, *Aestheticus.org* invited Efrain Arroyave, MD, who invited a group of prominent, board-certified aesthetic medical practitioners to collaborate on this book as coauthors. These coauthors are credited in their respective chapter(s).

Each patient is different and presents different considerations. Likewise, to some extent, physicians differ in the manner in which they approach their patients. Thus, the rationale for the different aspects of patient care expressed in this book simply represents the authors' preferences.

WHO CAN BENEFIT FROM THIS BOOK

- Student estheticians
- Cosmetologists
- Clinical estheticians
- Skin care specialists
- Nurses
- Spa personnel
- Aesthetic medical practitioners' staff
- Department store beauty consultants
- Pharmaceutical and product representatives to the aesthetic medical industry

- Massage therapists
- People considering cosmetic surgery

ACKNOWLEDGMENTS

Writing this book, much like raising a child, has been a community effort. As such, I would like to acknowledge this community. To begin with, this book would not have been possible without:

1. The board of directors and staff at Aestheticus.org (*Aesthetic Medical Education Resources, Inc.*).
2. The contributing, board-certified physicians who donated their valuable knowledge and time.
3. Cali Victoria Arroyave, who provided invaluable assistance in the preparation of the manuscript.
4. The following reviewers of the manuscript for their valuable observations and recommendations: Ms. Rosalie Rizzo, Ms. Ruthann Holloway, Ms. Jean Harrity, Ms. Sallie Deitz, Ms. LoriAnn Schell, and John A. Grossman, MD.
5. Ms. Sandra Fabian, director of operations for http://www.vitimmune.com, for the literature searches and amassing the more than 200 peer-reviewed articles that were used to write the chapter on oral antioxidants.
6. Ms. Cynthia Steele, research coordinator at the Biodoron Institute, for her invaluable typing and editorial assistance.
7. The following companies, individuals, and physicians who contributed graphics to this book:

   - Shippert Medical Technologies
   - Annette International
   - *American Journal of Cosmetic Surgery*
   - American Academy of Dermatology
   - Inamed Corporation
   - Liza Sims
   - Mary Jane Haake at Dermigraphics, LLC
   - Society of Permanent Cosmetic Professionals (SPCP)
   - ConBio Lasers
   - Allergan, Inc.
   - Vitimmune.com
   - Jeffrey S. Epstein, MD, FACS
   - Harry Sendzischew, MD
   - Mark G. Rubin, MD
   - Marjorie M. Grimm, CPCP
   - Judith E. Crowell, MD

About the Author

Efrain Arroyave, MD

Dr. Arroyave trained in plastic and reconstructive surgery at the Lahey Clinic and Boston University. In 1993 he cofounded the first *medical day spa* on Miami Beach. While in practice, he contributed to the medical literature, organized America Medical Association (AMA)-accredited continuing medical education (CME) courses on aesthetic medicine for physicians and nurses, was featured in several magazines throughout Latin America, produced and cohosted a cable television series on the latest in plastic and reconstructive surgery, produced a cable television series on aesthetic (cosmetic) medicine, and was a member of the American Society of Plastic Surgeons.

After sustaining a career-ending hand injury, Dr. Arroyave was the founder and Chief Executive Officer for a healthcare marketing firm specializing in promoting top medical specialists and medical centers to Latin Americans who come to the United States for their healthcare needs. Some such centers included: Massachusetts General Hospital, Texas Heart Institute, the Cleveland Clinic, and Mt. Sinai Medical Center. Dr. Arroyave was the founder, Chief Operating Officer, and Medical Director for medicinanews.com, the world's largest medical multimedia company, as well as serving as the editor-in-chief for *NEXOS*, the medical section of American Airlines' Spanish-Portuguese in-flight magazine. Dr. Arroyave later founded a business development company for the beauty industry. It was during this time that he began a relationship with *Aestheticus.org* (Aesthetic Medical Education Resources, Inc.), where he volunteers his time and knowledge to this worthwhile organization.

List of Contributors

Judith E. Crowell, MD
Voluntary Associate Professor, University
  of Miami
Department of Dermatology and Cutaneous
  Surgery
Miami, FL

Jeffrey S. Epstein, MD, FACS
Facial Plastic Surgeon
Miami, FL, and New York, NY

Marjorie M. Grimm, CPCP
Faces By Design
Santa Clara, CA, and Renton, WA

R. H. Keller, MD, MS, FACP
Immunologist
Hollywood, FL

Joel M. Levin, MD, FACS
Plastic and Reconstructive Surgeon
Chief, Department of Plastic Surgery
Baptist Hospital of Miami
Miami, FL

Alan Matarasso, MD
Clinical Associate Professor of Plastic Surgery
Albert Einstein College of Medicine
New York, NY

Mark G. Rubin, MD
Cosmetic Dermatologist
Beverly Hills, CA

Harry Sendzischew, MD, FACS
Vascular Surgeon
Medical Staff President
Mount Sinai Medical Center
Miami Beach, FL

Leslie H. Stevens, MD, FACS
Plastic and Reconstructive Surgeon
Beverly Hills, CA

Susanne S. Warfield
President and CEO
Paramedical Consultants, Inc.

Photo Credits

Milady would like to thank those who have graciously provided the following photos and images:

Figures 4–2a, 4–2b

Allergan, Inc.

Figures 4–3a, 4–3b, 6–1a, 6–1b, 7–1a, 7–1b, 7–4, 8–1a, 8–1b, 8–2a, 8–2b, 8–8a, 8–8b, 8–12, 9–1a, 9–1b, 9–3a, 9–3b, 9–7

American Academy of Dermatology

Figures 8–9a, 8–9b, 9–2a, 9–2b, 13–3a, 13–3b, 16–2, 19–3, 21–4

American Journal of Cosmetic Surgery

Figure 21–2

Annette International

Figures 8–4a, 8–4b, 8–5a, 8–5b, 8–6a, 8–6b, 8–7a, 8–7b, 8–10a, 8–10b

Hoya ConBio Medical and Dental Lasers

Figures 5–1a, 5–1b, 5–2a, 5–3a, 5–3b, 5–4a, 5–4b, 13–4, 17–3

Inamed Corporation

Figure 15–7, 17–4, 20–4, 21–3

Shippert Medical Technologies

Figures 8–3a, 8–3b, 8–11a, 8–11b
Judith E. Crowell, MD

Figures 13–1a, 13–1b, 13–2, 13–5a, 13–5b, 13–6, 13–7, 13–8, 13–9a, 13–9b
Jeffrey S. Epstein, MD, FACS

Figures 10–1a, 10–1b, 10–2a, 10–2b, 10–3a, 10–3b, 10–3c, 10–3d, 10–6
Marjorie M. Grimm, CPCP, Faces By Design

Figures 10–4a, 10–4b
Mary Jane Haake, Dermigraphics, LLC

Figures 12–1a, 12–1b
R. Emil Hecht, MD

Figures 11–4a, 11–4b, 14–3a, 14–3b, 17–5a, 17–5b
David Rappaport, MD, Plastic Surgeon, Park Avenue, NY

Figure 6–3
Mark G. Rubin, MD

Figures 9–4a, 9–4b, 9–5, 9–6
Harry Sendzischew, MD

Figures 10–5a, 10–5b
Liza Sims, Anchorage, Alaska

Figure 6–2
Larry Hamill Photography

All other illustrations created by Graphic World Inc.

Section One

General Information

Chapter 1

Enter the "Clinical" Skin Care Specialists

■ Susanne S. Warfield

There are more than 78 million "baby boomers" in the United States, and their ranks are joined by the more than 10,000 people who turn 50 every day. A good number of this population enjoy a higher disposable income and tend to be more demanding. As this population group lives longer, they seek facilities with qualified professionals to make them look and feel younger longer. Add to this the growing demand for aesthetic procedures in younger people, and it is not surprising that during the past decade we have witnessed an explosion—and convergence—of **aesthetic medicine**, medical spas, antiaging medicine, and longevity centers.

As products, procedures, and techniques for skin care become more scientifically based and the level of complexity increases with impressive results, the media as well as the aesthetic medical industry has inspired the public to, once again, believe in the "fountain of youth." Thus, in addition to aesthetic surgical procedures, many patients are demanding comprehensive skin care from spas, **medispas**, and **aesthetic medical practitioners**.

The skin care specialist or *esthetician*—as they are licensed in most states—is now entering into the clinical setting to provide ancillary services under the direct supervision of the physician.

According to the most comprehensive survey to date of U.S. physicians and surgeons by the American Society for Aesthetic Plastic Surgery, from 1997 to 2004, there has been a 465 percent increase in the total number of cosmetic surgeries/procedures. Surgical procedures increased by 118 percent, and nonsurgical procedures increased by 764 percent. Approximately 46 percent of these cosmetic surgeries/

Esthetician and aesthetician are synonymous terms.

procedures were performed in physicians' offices, 29 percent in free-standing surgery centers, and 24 percent in hospitals.

It should therefore not be surprising that *aesthetic medical practitioners* can now be found in a new breed of spa facilities called **medical spas**, or *medispas*, which is a spa-type facility that operates under the full-time, on-site supervision of a licensed healthcare professional. The facility operates within the scope of practice of its staff and offers traditional, complementary, and alternative health practices and treatments in a spa-like setting. Many aesthetic medical practitioners are employing skin care specialists who come from the ranks of dermatology and plastic surgery nurses, estheticians, and specially trained medical assistants. If licensure is required, practitioners working within a medical spa will be governed by their appropriate licensing board.

Accordingly, to optimize surgical and nonsurgical skin care regimens, most aesthetic medical practitioners are more diligent about the study and application of skin care products, equipment, and techniques. These physicians now select skin care products suited for each individual patient's skin type, maintenance needs, and goals of the planned aesthetic procedures/surgeries. Understanding their time constraints, aesthetic medical practitioners often employ or work closely with skin care specialists. Consequently, there has been a parallel demand for a new breed of skin care professionals.

Although the aesthetic physician's skill is the first assurance of quality results for aesthetic medical procedures, adding a properly trained and experienced skin care specialist to a practice is a smart move, not only for patient care but also for patient satisfaction. In-house skin care specialists, in concert with the physician's treatment plan, can provide optimal preprocedure and postprocedure skin care, as well as offer select spa-type skin care modalities and maintenance skin care regimens. The development of a good rapport between the physician and the "properly trained" esthetician is essential for this relationship to truly work.

At first the esthetician may not have the educational background one would expect, and the physician needs to ascertain what other assets the skin care specialist would bring to the practice during the interview process. By virtue of their services, added personal attention, and bonding with patients, the esthetician can contribute to patient retention, patient referrals, and passive marketing. Marketing to the cosmetic patient greatly differs from the client in a salon and spa setting, and the ability to share open communication between physician and esthetician is a must!

Interestingly, more than 15 years ago, most physicians and the public considered nonmedical skin care by estheticians as "fluff"; dermatologists aside, up until the late 1980s, most aesthetic medical/

surgical practitioners did not offer preoperative and/or postoperative skin care.

The aesthetic medical industry is calling for skin care specialists with advanced training and/or experience in working with aesthetic medical patients, and alliances are being formed between estheticians and medical aesthetic practitioners at all levels. It goes without saying that in a clinical setting the advice and services provided by these skin care specialists runs parallel to and under the direct supervision of the physician.

Although skin care specialists are in demand by aesthetic medical practitioners, spas, medispas, and resorts looking to offer their clients the best in skin care services, an education lag currently exists in training clinical skin care specialists.

Because of the recent increase and demand for estheticians (the most prominent technicians in skin care), let us consider their education requirements, which have come a long way in the past 20 years. Thankfully, today efforts are well on their way to bringing the educational needs to the market's demand for "clinical" skin care specialists. Some states have begun to set progressive standards for the industry—Utah has a two-tier licensing program for estheticians, which includes a master esthetician program (do not confuse this with a master's degree from a college or university). The Florida College of Natural Health, a leader in training estheticians and massage therapists, also has a multitier esthetician program with a 1,000 hour "advanced paramedical skin care course" and even an associate of science degree for estheticians looking to expand their knowledge and meet market demands. Students are taught available treatments for dealing with wrinkles, sun damage, pigmentation, acne, and so forth.

The formation of **NCEA** (www.ncea.tv) in January 2000 has helped organize the skin care industry and build consensus to present a unified voice for lobbying efforts and they have now set national standards for training estheticians. The process of getting new legislation passed in each state will be a 4- to 10-year path. The NCEA is a coalition of estheticians, manufacturers, distributors, and associations that have come together and taken responsibility for the industry and have set a basic esthetician program of 600 hours and an advanced 1,200 hour esthetician program. There is currently only one state that has a two-tier licensing system of 1,200 hours total; a half-dozen other states have more than 600 hours of training but not quite a total of 1,200 hours. To have national endorsement, and the ability of the esthetician or skin care specialist to cross state lines, each state will have to standardize their educational and licensing requirements.

Many professional skin care organizations provide education to skin care professionals to work in a variety of settings, including the Society of Dermatology Skin Care Specialists (www.sdss.tv), the

Physicians should only employ estheticians, because paying them as independent contractors is illegal (Internal Revenue Service rules). Further, there are liability issues if the medical facility "rents" rooms to nonmedical practitioners.

Aesthetic medical practitioners include cosmetic dermatologists, plastic surgeons (plastic and reconstructive surgeons), facial plastic and reconstructive surgeons (otolaryngologists), as well as some other specialists who provide services in aesthetic medicine.

Society of Plastic Surgical Skin Care Specialists (www.surgery.org/skincare), the Medical Spa Society (www.medicalspasociety.com), and the International Medical Spa Association (www.medicalspaassociation.org), to name a few. For a complete list of professional organizations within the skin care industry, go to www.ncea.tv/associationmembers.html.

A better understanding of the medical/surgical side of the aesthetic industry is just as important as knowing skin care products, equipment, and application techniques. Enhanced knowledge of the medical side of the aesthetic industry would allow estheticians and other skin care specialists to better integrate their services and product knowledge into the clinical side of skin care. Accordingly, the NCEA has recommended the following additions:

1. The basic 600-hour course should include education in common surgical and nonsurgical procedures in dermatology and plastic surgery.
2. The advanced course should include:
   a. increased medical terminology and interactions with aesthetic medical practitioners to encourage a better understand of medically treated conditions of the skin.
   b. familiarization of prescription and over-the-counter drugs commonly used by aesthetic medical practitioners.

Chapter 2

Understanding Wound Healing

With a surface area of approximately 22 square feet in adults, and accounting for approximately one-sixth the weight of the human body, the skin is the largest organ in the body. The epidermis contributes to the skin's protective function as a barrier (e.g., mechanical injury, thermal injury, chemical injury, and infectious organisms, to which it is constantly exposed). There is, therefore, a constant **sloughing** of old or damaged epidermal cells, which requires continual regeneration of the epidermis from the **stratum germinativum**, the deepest layer of the epidermis. These newly formed epidermal cells mature and become **keratinized** as they move to the surface.

The skin is composed of two layers, the epidermis and the dermis. The epidermis receives its nourishment and physical support from the underlying dermis; the dermis derives its strength from collagen and cross-linked fibrous protein that stretch and relax with age and sun damage. When the integrity of the skin is interrupted, a complex orchestration of cellular and physiologic events is triggered.

SUPERFICIAL INJURIES (EPIDERMAL INJURY)

Reepithelialization is essential when the skin surface is violated by a scrape, superficial burn, or incision. Within 12 hours of the damage to the epidermis, epithelial cells from the wound margin and the **pilosebaceous units** (Figure 2–1) begin to migrate to repair the damage. As dryness impairs efficient migration of the epithelium, it is essential to keep the wound moist as it heals.

Figure 2–1

The hair follicle or pilosebaceous unit.

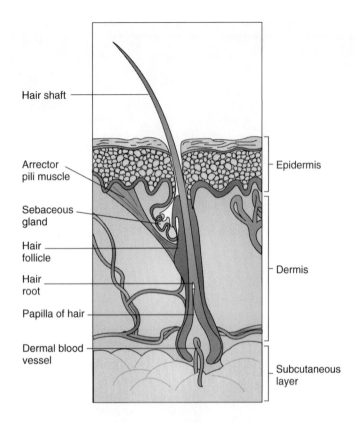

Hair shaft

Arrector
pili muscle

Sebaceous
gland

Hair
follicle

Hair
root

Papilla of hair

Dermal blood
vessel

Epidermis

Dermis

Subcutaneous
layer

DEEPER WOUNDS (EPIDERMIS AND DERMIS)

Wounds that extend into the connective tissue of the dermis cause damage to the microvascular system and invoke a more complex healing process. The dermis has two layers: the **papillary layer** (upper) and the **reticular layer** (lower). The papillary layer can heal from injuries without scarring; however, when the reticular layer is damaged, *scars* may result (Figure 2–2).

At this level of injury, the healing process is divided into three overlapping phases: inflammatory, proliferative, and migratory.

Inflammatory Phase

To establish some **hemostasis** immediately after an injury at this level, there is a period of **vasoconstriction** that lasts several minutes. This is followed by a couple of days of **vasodilatation** that allows a buildup of the necessary cells and protein to repair deeper wounds. During this phase **fibroblasts** are stimulated to regulate the production of collagen (Figure 2–3).

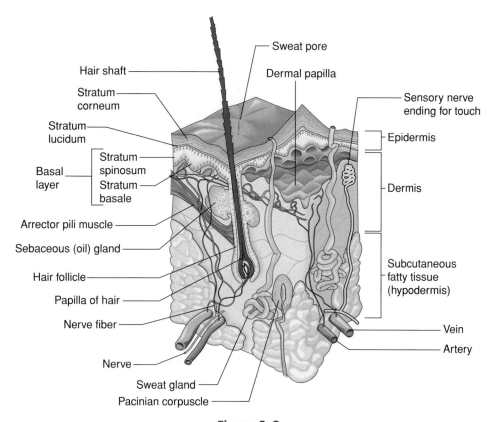

Figure 2–2

Cross-section of the skin.

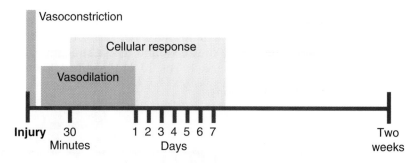

Figure 2–3

Inflammatory phase.

Figure 2–4

Proliferative phase.

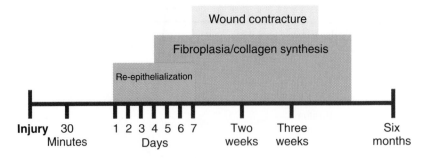

Proliferative Phase

The proliferative phase usually begins about one week after the injury or incision (Figure 2–4). During this phase there is an *increase in vascularity* of the wound to provide critical nutrients and oxygen to sustain the metabolism of the healing wound, particularly the deposition of collagen. *Wound contracture* begins at the tail end of the proliferative phase.

Approximating the wound margin with sutures, staples, butterfly stitches, or a superficial adhesive agent will minimize the granulation tissue and accelerate wound healing. This is known as *healing by primary intention.*

The natural (unrepaired) process of wound healing is termed *healing by secondary intention.* In these wounds, wound contracture can account for up to 40 percent decrease in wound size. In contrast, superficial injuries that involve only the epidermis will contract very little, if at all.

Maturation Phase (Remodeling)

This, the final phase of wound healing, is characterized by an increase in strength without increase in collagen content (Figure 2–5).

By three to six weeks the maximum amount of collagen has been laid down in the wound; however, this collagen is then remodeled and aligned to maximize wound **tensile strength**. During this phase, special enzymes serve to ensure that the breakdown and production

Figure 2–5

Maturation phase.

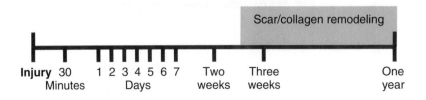

Figure 2–6

Wound tensile strength over time.

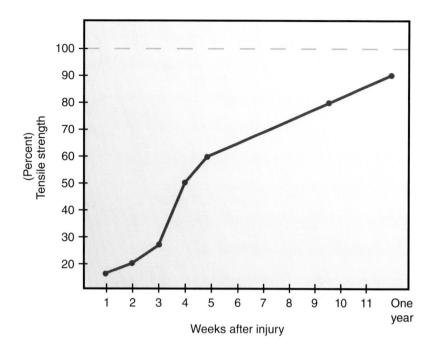

of collagen is balanced to keep a constant amount of collagen in the wound. This equilibrium serves to maximize mature configurations of the resulting collagen, which allows cross-linking and alignment in the wound along the axis of maximum tension, thereby increasing tensile strength.

Within one month after the injury, the tensile strength of the wound will have increased to about 40 percent of the preinjury tensile strength. This tensile strength will continue to increase for up to one year postinjury; however, the repaired wound will never be as strong as the preinjured skin—it usually peaks at approximately 80 percent of its original strength (Figure 2–6).

SUTURE (STITCHES) TECHNIQUES

Suturing, or stitching, is a method of wound repair using thin thread made of different materials. They can be absorbable or nonabsorbable. Unlike the nonabsorbable sutures, the absorbable sutures do not need to be removed. Sutures may be placed individually ("interrupted") or as a single continuous series of loops ("running").

Radiation and the Skin

Depending on the radiation used, the amount administered, and other factors, the skin in the vicinity of the treated area may become red, sensitive, or easily irritated in the days, weeks, and months during and after radiation treatment for cancer. The skin may swell or droop or the texture may change. Most symptoms of skin damage are temporary, although a person may get *permanent* changes in skin tone or texture.

Figure 2–7

Simple interrupted sutures.

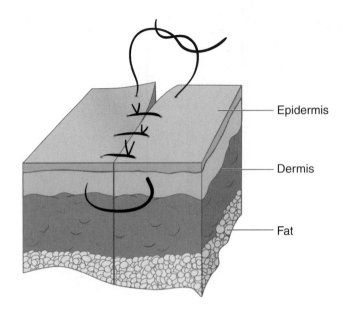

Epidermis

Dermis

Fat

Simple Suture

This is the most basic of the suture techniques, involving the approximation of the tissue margins with "interrupted" *single loops* of sutures (Figure 2–7). Superficial, *simple,* or *running* sutures are usually nonabsorbable, and sub-Q sutures and sutures used to close **mucosa** are usually absorbable.

Buried Sutures

This form is simply an inverted form of the simple suture technique that is placed beneath the skin or mucosa (i.e., the knot is placed at the deepest point of the loop). As the skin is closed, the "buried" suture is no longer visible. This technique is often referred to as "**subcuticular**" or "**sub-Q**" (Figure 2–8). Based on the injury, they can be placed as "interrupted" or "running" (continuous).

Running Sutures

This technique uses one continuous suture in a series of "running loops" that is held with a knot at the beginning and end of the incision line. They can be superficial or buried (Figure 2–9).

Nonsuture Wound Closures

Wound closure can also be achieved by material other than sutures (e.g., skin staples, adhesive tapes ["butterfly"], and tissue adhesives).

Figure 2–8
Buried sutures.

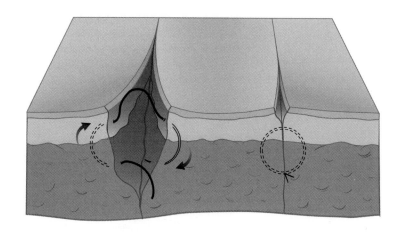

Figure 2–9
Running subcuticular sutures.

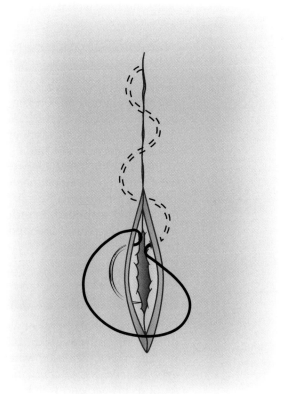

Large wounds often require both buried, absorbable sutures as well as superficial, nonabsorbable sutures.

Table 2–1   Recommended Suture Removal Based on Location

Suture Location	Suture Size	Recommended Removal
Scalp	3–0/4–0	7 to 12 days
Face	4–0 to 6–0	3 to 7 days
Ear	5–0/6–0	4 to 6 days
Neck	4–0/5–0	5 to 7 days
Chest		
Back	4–0/5–0	6 to 12 days
Abdomen		
Arms and legs	3–0 to 5–0	6 to 14 days
Oral cavity	4–0	
	(Absorbable)	Absorbed

Note: the higher the number of the suture material, the thinner it is.

SUTURE REMOVAL

The appropriate time for suture removal varies with the area of the body and how well it is healing (Table 2–1).

DRESSINGS AND TOPICAL OINTMENTS

The wound surface needs to be kept clean and moist, while looking for any signs of infection. Dressings are applied to protect the wound from contaminants, reduce pain, and absorb **exudates** as the wound heals.

A topical antibiotic ointment may assist in healing and keeping the wound surface moist to aid in the migration of migratory **keratinocytes** as they reepithelialize the wound. Either a light coat may be applied with semiporous, nonadherent gauze to absorb exudates or a more generous amount may be applied alone. The ointment should be removed and reapplied according to the physician's instructions. This also gives the patient an opportunity to cleanse the wound and check for signs of infection.

BATHING

During the initial phases of wound healing, the **sebaceous gland's** production of protective skin oils will decrease, resulting in decreased protection and increased water absorption by the healing tissue; however, *minimal risk of* **contamination** is seen with *"brief immersion"* of wounds in soap and water after 24 hours.

SMOKING AND HEALING

Nicotine decreases blood circulation in the skin and thus impairs blood flow to the tiny vessels that supply the dermis, causing delayed wound healing or complications such as tissue loss and subsequent scarring. Therefore, smokers are instructed not to smoke for several weeks before and after the procedure.

SUN EXPOSURE AND WOUND HEALING

It has been reported that greater than 50 percent of our exposure to the sun occurs before most people reach their 18th birthday. The daily exposure, regardless of duration, creates a *cumulative effect* that inevitably results in signs of accelerated aging. Hyperpigmentation of a scar or wound may be avoided by avoiding sun exposure. Thus, after 7 to 10 days postoperative, sunscreen with SPF 15 or greater should be used for approximately 6 months. Patients who have had *head, face,* and/or *neck* surgery should also wear wide rim hats and sunglasses immediately postoperative.

SPF represents the ability of an agent to delay sun-induced redness of the skin. Theoretically, a person who applies a sunscreen with an SPF of 10 (on exposed body parts) could remain in the sun 10 times longer without incurring visible skin redness; sunscreen with an SPF of 15 (on exposed body parts) could remain in the sun 15 times longer without incurring visible skin redness, and so forth.

Skin Aging

Although scientists have yet to completely understand the *intrinsic factors* relating to skin aging, they have identified UV radiation, lifestyle, smoking, alcohol, and poor nutrition as *extrinsic factors* that contribute to skin aging. Skin aging is also related to genetics and age-related buildup of **free radicals.** Signs of skin aging include wrinkles, blotchiness, roughened texture, a sallowed coloration, and sagging.

Fitzpatrick's Classification of Skin Types

Skin Type	Skin Color	Description
I	White, pale, or freckled (extremely fair skin)	Always burns, never tans
II	White, pale with beige tint (fair skin)	Usually burns, slightly tans
III	White to olive skin	Sometimes burns, mostly tans
IV	Brown	Rarely burns, always tans
V	Dark brown (moderately pigmented)	Very rarely burns
VI	Black	Never burns

Local Factors That Impair Wound Healing

Surgical Technique

- Rough handling of tissue may crush the wound edges and devitalize the tissue.
- Highly reactive suture material may increase inflammation and delay wound healing.
- Overly tight skin sutures may decrease blood flow through the capillaries in the dermis and cause tissue loss.

Hematoma Formation

- Excessive bleeding can mechanically disrupt wound closure.
- Hematoma separates healing tissue from blood supply.
- Hematomas are an excellent culture medium for bacteria.

Wound Care

- Dryness of a wound will impair epithelial migration.
- Scabs inhibit healing and increase the distance epithelial cells must travel.

Foreign Bodies

- Foreign bodies prolong inflammation by attracting inflammatory cells.
- Necrotic tissue and pus contain proteolytic enzymes that damage cells and slow the healing process.
- Infection, which is defined as more than 10,000 organisms/gram of tissue, impairs healing by attracting inflammatory cells that compete for oxygen and nutrients, thereby damaging the cells/tissue.

Low Oxygen Delivery to the Tissue

- Decreases tissue growth
- Increases susceptibility to infection

Systemic Factors That Impair Wound Healing

Smoking

- Causes vasoconstriction, which decreases blood flow to wound
- Carbon monoxide preferentially binds hemoglobin, thereby reducing the delivery of oxygen to the wound

Circulatory Disease (atherosclerosis, congestive heart failure)

- Decreases delivery of oxygen, nutrients, and inflammatory mediators to the wound

Diabetes Mellitus

- Affects tiny blood vessels and thereby diminishes oxygen delivery to the tissues
- Insulin deficiency decreases white blood cell function
- Insulin deficiency impairs collagen synthesis
- Vitamin A supplements can decrease the effects of diabetes on wound healing

Diseases That Can Cause *Immunosuppression*

- Diabetes mellitus
- Liver failure
- Kidney failure
- Asplenism (no spleen)
- Alcoholism

Systemic Corticosteroids and Other Immunosuppressants

- Decreases the functioning of several cell types important in the healing
- Decreases epithelialization
- Decreases collagen production by fibroblasts
- Systemic vitamin A may reverse steroidal effect by promoting release of inflammatory mediators

Nutritional Deficiencies Such as Occur with Cancer or Alcoholism

- Protein deficiencies impair the proliferative phase of wound healing.
- Fatty acid deficiencies impair wound healing.
- Vitamin deficiencies (A, B, and C) impair wound healing.

Aging

- Fibroblastic activity decreases with age, reducing wound tensile strength.
- Increased proteolytic activity with aging results in greater tissue breakdown.
- Increased incidence of pulmonary and circulatory disease (see above)

Chapter 3

Preprocedure and Postprocedure Concerns

Although it is commonly recognized that preprocedure and postprocedure skin care can improve the healing and final result of aesthetic medical procedures, the number and efficacy of available skin care treatments is beyond the scope of this book. Rather, in keeping with the intent of this book, the authors will focus on the preprocedure and postprocedure concerns in caring for patients undergoing surgical and/or nonsurgical aesthetic procedures.

The best candidates for any cosmetic procedure are healthy, emotionally stable people with realistic expectations. In as much as the skin is the largest organ in the human body and because it is the primary organ of interest in most aesthetic procedures, it warrants a thorough examination. Before any aesthetic procedure, it is essential to obtain a medical history and perform a physical examination that includes a thorough and proper examination of the skin.

PREPROCEDURE CONCERNS

Medical and Surgical History

With *any* type of surgical or nonsurgical procedure, the medical and surgical history of the patient must be carefully noted because **systemic** (and local) factors can affect anesthesia and wound healing.

Has the patient had previous surgery or problems with previous surgeries? Has the patient ever had a reaction to anesthesia? Is there a history of **blood clots** or bleeding problems? Is there a history of wound healing problems or tendency toward scarring? Is there a history of high blood pressure, heart disease, lung disease, diabetes, and so forth? Has the patient experienced blotchy skin pigmentation with pregnancy, birth control pills, or sun exposure? Is there a history of infectious skin diseases and/or herpes cold sores? Is there a history of skin cancer or other types of cancer?

Social History

The physician will want to be aware of the patient's social habits that may interfere with surgery or the healing process.

Does the patient smoke? If so, how many packs per day, and for how long? What is the patient's history to sun exposure? Is the patient a surfer? Does the patient spend much time on the beach without sun protection? Does the patient drink excessive amounts of alcohol?

Family History

Because some disease processes are genetic or familial, obtaining a family history often brings up concerns for the physician to consider.

Are there any family members with cancer? Have any family members ever had a problem with unusual bleeding, wound healing, or excessive scarring? Have any family members ever had problems with surgery or a reaction to anesthesia?

Review of Systems

Most patients do not know what is important to reveal before a surgical procedure; therefore, the physician will ask specific questions about symptoms associated with certain diseases. For example, someone with heart or lung disease may experience shortness of breath (**SOB**) at rest and/or with exertion; a history of chest pain at rest or with exertion may indicate heart disease; frequent urination may indicate a urinary tract infection or diabetes, and so forth.

Medications and Nutritional Supplements

There are literally hundreds of prescription medications, over-the-counter medications, and nutritional supplements that can interfere with the normal clotting mechanism and should be avoided before surgery. Physicians routinely screen patients for these.

Aspirin products, vitamin E, Motrin-type medications (NSAIDs), Cox II inhibitors (i.e., Vioxx, Celebrex, and so forth), and many other medications should be discontinued sometime before elective surgery. Further, many nutritional supplements can interfere with normal blood clotting. Eight commonly used nutritional supplements that interfere with the normal clotting mechanism are *echinacea, ephedra, garlic, gingko biloba, ginseng, kava, St. John's wart,* and *valerian.*

Allergies

Because the patient may receive some form of pain medication or antibiotic, it is important to know if the patient has ever experienced an allergic reaction to a specific drug or class of drugs (e.g., penicillin, sulfa drugs, codeine, and so forth). Is the patient allergic to latex or certain adhesive skin tape?

Laboratory Tests (Labs)

Not all medical or surgical procedures require a panel of blood tests. Some do not require any lab tests. The physician makes this determination based on the procedure, type of anesthesia, and the general health of the individual patient. In general, if any incisions are involved, a clotting study is indicated (i.e., **PT, PTT,** and **bleeding time**).

X-rays

Depending on the patient's age and family history, the physician may require certain radiographic exams (e.g., chest X-ray [CXR], facial X-rays, a mammogram with certain types of breast surgery, and so forth).

Physical Examination of the Skin

After a complete history and physical examination to evaluate the overall condition of the patient, the patient's skin should be thoroughly examined for the following:

- Underlying support structure in the cutaneous area of concern to the patient
- Signs of infection (e.g., **erythema** or redness of the skin)
- The state of hydration
- Uniformity of coloration and texture
- Tumors
- Ulcers or wounds
- Oiliness
- Elasticity

Assessment for Aesthetic Procedure

The physician must determine if the patient has realistic expectations and whether the procedure will meet the patient's goal—with minimal risks. The physician may actually suggest a different procedure(s) than the one requested by the patient (e.g., patients who want dermabrasion of their face may actually fare better with a face peel). Or, the physician may suggest an ancillary procedure (e.g., a chin implant to balance a **rhinoplasty** in patients with a weak chin).

Preprocedure Discussion with the Patient

Once the physician is satisfied that the procedure is indicated and that the patient has realistic expectations, he or she will discuss the procedure, the preparation, and what to expect after the procedure. In addition, patients may be advised to have a friend or family member stay with them for the first 24 to 48 hours postprocedure to assist them with routine activities.

Patients are advised of the sun's effects on healing and scarring. The patient is also informed that healing is a gradual process. Finally, a **consent form** is signed and photographs are taken.

Risks and Complications

No medical or surgical aesthetic procedure is without risks. However, when performed by a properly trained and experienced *aesthetic medical practitioner*, most complications known to be associated with aesthetic medicine are infrequent and usually minor. When patients remain compliant with their physician's instructions they can minimize certain risks, making the overall experience much smoother.

Major complications tend to be rare and can be minimized by adhering to the five pillars of safety as follows:

1. Safe surgeon
2. Safe anesthesiologist
3. Safe facility
4. Safe surgical staff
5. Compliant patient

Preprocedure Instructions to the Patient

Once the procedure(s) is/are decided on, the patient is given written preprocedure and postprocedure instructions particular for any given procedure(s). Depending on the individual patient's health status, the instructions may include guidelines regarding diet, alcohol intake, smoking, and which medications to take or avoid. Depending on the procedure and/or anesthesia, patients may be instructed not to eat or drink anything after midnight the day before surgery.

Patients are instructed to immediately notify the physician if they develop a cold sore (fever blister), cold, or infection of any kind before surgery, as the procedure may need to be postponed.

Transportation to and from the Procedure

Whether the procedure is done on an outpatient or inpatient basis, the patient should arrange transportation to and from the surgical facility.

Skin Preparation Before the Procedure

Today, *aesthetic medical practitioners* understand that certain skin care products can optimize surgical and nonsurgical aesthetic procedures, both preprocedure and postprocedure. Like selecting a surgical instrument, physicians and/or their skin care specialists may select skin care products specifically suited for each particular patient's skin type and needs. Although discussion of such products and/or their efficacy is beyond the scope of this book, depending on the type of procedure as well as the patient's skin type, the skin should be brought to its optimal health before aesthetic surgery. Some forms of **skin resurfacing** may benefit with pretreatments.

Preprocedure Medications

Depending on the patient's health, the procedure to be performed, and the physician's preferences, some patients may be given oral and/or intravenous antibiotics before the procedure. Appropriate nutritional supplements and antioxidants may also be recommended.

POSTPROCEDURE CONCERNS

Postprocedure Antibiotics

Depending on the patient's health, the procedure performed, and the physician's preferences, some patients may be given oral antibiotics and/or antibiotic ointment for several days postoperative.

Postprocedure Instructions

Postprocedure activity will depend on the procedure(s), the healing progress exhibited by the patient, and the physician's preferences. Bathing, hair care, and makeup instructions will depend on the procedure and satisfactory wound healing.

Patients may be instructed to avoid sun exposure and extreme heat for several days postoperative, particularly when superficial

sensory nerves have been interrupted. They are also encouraged to make healthy lifestyle changes, including stopping smoking, eating a healthy diet, and drinking plenty of water. Finally the patient is given follow-up and wound care instructions. "Soaking" in bathtubs should be avoided before complete reepithelialization of the wound/incision(s) or until cleared by the treating physician; "quick" showering is usually acceptable after most procedures.

Postprocedure Skin Care

An individualized skin care regimen may be designed to maximize the results of the aesthetic procedure. The prescribed regimen will depend on the procedure(s) performed, patient's skin type, and goals. Some common treatments can include:

- Low concentration peels
- Retinol creams
- Toners
- Moisturizers
- Humectants
- Vitamin creams
- Sunscreen
- Antioxidants and other nutritional supplements
- Cleansing and a gentle lymphatic massage with essential oils
- Proper makeup application to cover any bruising

Section Two

Nonsurgical Aesthetic Procedures

Chapter 4

Botulinum Toxin
Botox

■ Judith E. Crowell, MD

Causes of Dynamic Facial Wrinkles

One of the main causes of dynamic facial wrinkles—the **glabellar** furrows, **crow's feet,** and forehead wrinkles—are the result of "purse string" gathering of the skin over the muscles associated with repeated facial expressions (i.e., *frontalis* muscles, *procerus* muscles, *corrugator* muscles, and *orbiclaris oculi* and *orbiclaris oris* muscles [Figure 4–1]). The axis of these wrinkles tend to be perpendicular to the action of the underlying facial muscle. Other factors that contribute to wrinkle formation are genes, sun damage, hormones, and nutrition.

Botulinum toxin is a biologic toxin that is produced by **Clostridium botulinum**, a bacteria responsible for a life-threatening form of food poisoning. For more than 30 years, *purified botulinum toxin* has been used as a therapeutic agent to treat noncosmetic medical conditions such as "lazy eye" and "blinking ticks." Then, in 1987, dermatologists pioneered its use for the temporary treatment of facial wrinkles caused by repetitive, long-term contractions of certain facial muscle. Two forms of botulinum toxins are used for this purpose—Botox and **Myobloc**. Both are purified biologic toxins that block nerve signals to the muscle. Today Botox injections (for wrinkles) is the most common cosmetic procedure in the United States, representing about 25 percent of all nonsurgical cosmetic procedures.

INDICATIONS

- "Glabellar" lines between the eyebrows and on the bridge of the nose (Figure 4–2A)
- Squint lines or "crows feet" at the corners of the eyes
- The forehead horizontal ("frown") (Figure 4–3A)
- "Smoker's" lip lines (see Chapter 8, Figure 8–9A or Chapter 5, Figure 5–3A)

In the neck area (although not a wrinkle), the **turkey neck** caused by platysma muscle bands can usually be softened with botulinum toxin. This toxin has limited use for the treatment of "smile lines" and

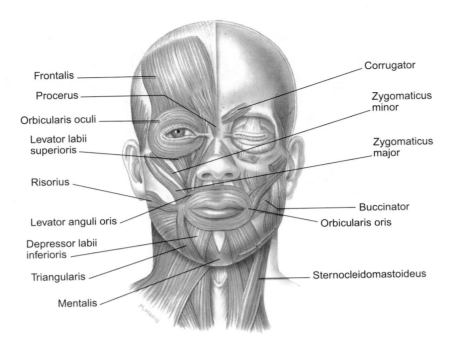

Figure 4–1

Facial muscles.

Frontalis
Procerus
Orbicularis oculi
Levator labii superioris
Risorius
Levator anguli oris
Depressor labii inferioris
Triangularis
Mentalis

Corrugator
Zygomaticus minor
Zygomaticus major
Buccinator
Orbicularis oris
Sternocleidomastoideus

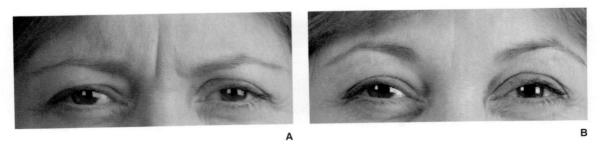

A

B

Figure 4–2

A, Glabellar lines. B, Glabellar lines—postinjection. Reprinted with the permission of Allergan Corporation. All rights reserved.

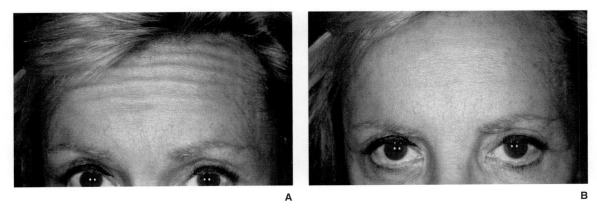

A B

Figure 4–3

A, Frowning. B, Frowning postinjection. Reprinted with the permission of the American Academy of Dermatology. All rights reserved.

wrinkles on the upper lip because the muscle action in these areas is needed for important functions such as smiling, eating, and talking.

MECHANISM OF ACTION AND TARGET TISSUES

It is not known whether injection of botulinum toxin has any effect on a fetus. Therefore, pregnant women should postpone this procedure until cleared by their obstetrician.

Botulinum toxin works by blocking nerve impulses to targeted facial muscles, which prevents contraction of the muscle. By injecting very tiny amounts into a specific facial muscle, only the neuromuscular impulse to that muscle will be temporarily blocked, causing a local (paralysis) relaxation and weakness. Thus, patients are no longer able to tighten and contract these muscles in a manner that creates the wrinkles associated with squinting and stressful concentration. The dynamic wrinkles and lines that lie immediately over the target muscle(s) gradually smooth out from disuse, and new creases are prevented from forming. With proper injection placement and technique, other muscles, like those needed to raise the eyebrows, are not affected, so a natural expression is maintained.

The toxin causes the target muscle(s) to relax within 24 to 72 hours, and the full effect is usually seen by 2 weeks after injection. Initially the effects typically last about 3 to 4 months before the muscle action gradually returns. Thus, the average patient will require reinjection at 3- to 4-month intervals. With repeated treatments, **atrophy** of the muscle may occur, and the results tend to last a little longer. Eventually, most patients require treatments only once or twice a year to maintain their desired appearance.

PREPROCEDURE CONSIDERATIONS

During the initial consultation, patients will need to discuss their concerns so that the physician can formulate the appropriate treatment plan.

Anesthesia

Anesthesia is rarely needed, but sedatives and topical numbing agents may occasionally be used. Some physicians may apply a mild analgesic cream to the area approximately 30 minutes before treatment.

PROCEDURE/TECHNIQUES

Toxin treatments can be performed in the doctor's office or in a surgical suite, and all injections should be performed using sterile techniques. After the physician identifies the target facial muscles that correspond to the areas of concern, the patient is asked to activate those muscles in order to plan the exact location of the injection. The physician will then use a tiny needle to inject a small amount of botulinum toxin directly into the muscle(s).

To attain the desired results and avoid unwanted results, the injections must be very precise. Injecting the toxin is an art (e.g., if the brow is injected too low, the eyelids may droop), but a strategically placed injection(s) will cause the brow to rise. Also, the shape of the eyebrow can be molded with strategic injections: women might prefer an arched eyebrow, whereas men might prefer a flat eyebrow. Thus, injections of botulinum toxin must be performed by a physician who understands the complex anatomy, **physiology**, and function(s) of the more than 40 muscles of the face.

The actual treatment is well tolerated and takes just a few minutes with no "down time" or prolonged recovery period. Depending on the number of injections needed, the treatment may take 10 to 30 minutes. Treatment with botulinum toxin is a very simple procedure, which allows the patient to return home immediately after the injections.

DRESSINGS AND WOUND CARE

Usually no dressings are needed. Patients should not touch the treated area, bend over, or lie down for at least four to six hours; doing so may cause the toxin to spread to nearby muscles, creating unwanted results. However, patients are instructed to use the muscles being treated to help the toxin diffuse through these muscles.

Sutures

None.

Bathing and Hair Care

Bathing and hair care can usually resume immediately after the procedure. However, patients should avoid touching facial muscles for at least six hours postinjection.

Makeup

Makeup may be worn the day after injections, but care should be taken to avoid pressing or massaging the area for up to six hours. If the upper third of the face was treated, it is safe to apply lipstick.

POSTPROCEDURE SKIN/TISSUE CHANGES

Side effects are minimal and typically relate to the local injection. Some patients may experience slight, short-term bruising at the injection site. The bruising is usually minimal and can be easily camouflaged with makeup. Soreness, although uncommon, may occur around the injection site. A temporary headache is not uncommon after injections in the forehead area, especially after the first treatment.

Other possible side effects include local numbness, swelling, or a burning sensation during injection. In rare instances, patients may develop temporary weakness of the neighboring muscles, a temporary droopy brow or eyelid, or temporary, slightly skewed facial expressions.

All of these possible effects are likely to be mild and temporary and, in most cases, do not significantly limit routine activities. Fortunately, these side effects are short term, lasting only a few weeks at the most. Some can be corrected with additional skillfully placed toxin. Time will reverse any unwanted side effects that may occur from the treatment.

A small percentage of patients are reported to experience no improvement at all. It is believed that these patients have had a mild case of botulinum poisoning in the past and have developed antibodies to the toxin.

Scars

None.

Long experience has proven botulinum toxin to be safe. Most complications are likely to be mild and temporary and can be avoided with proper injection techniques.

Uses for Botulinum Toxin to Treat Excess Sweating

Excessive sweating can be treated with injections of botulinum toxin directly into the axilla, the palms, or soles of the feet. The toxin paralyzes the sweat glands, which are responsible for excessive perspiration.

POSTPROCEDURE ACTIVITIES

Some physicians may recommend certain facial exercises to optimize the desired result. Patients are cautioned not to touch the area that was treated for at least 4 to 6 hours after injection. Doing so may cause the toxin to spread to other nearby muscles, creating unwanted results. Patients should avoid lying down or leaning over (head downward) for 4 to 6 hours after the injections, and they should also avoid exercise and strenuous activities for the first 24 hours after injections. After that time, they should be able to resume their normal activities.

SOME RISKS AND POSSIBLE COMPLICATIONS

The following are some risks that may occur:

- Temporary weakness of the neighboring muscles
- Temporary **ptosis** (drooping) of the eyelid(s)
- Temporary droopy brow
- Pointed raised (Spock-like) eyebrows

Chapter 5

Injectable Fillers

■ Mark G. Rubin, MD

Injectable fillers are a popular nonsurgical cosmetic procedure used to plump up wrinkles and facial creases, furrows, "sunken" cheeks, skin depressions, and some types of scars. They can also add fullness to the lips and cheeks. As more materials become available to use, there is more use of these fillers to help contour faces and increase volume in entire areas, rather than to just fill in a wrinkle or scar. See Table 5–1 for a partial list of available fillers.

There are many different types of *injectable fillers* currently available in the United States. They can be divided into several different groups, including animal derived, nonanimal derived, dermal fillers, subcutaneous fillers, and bioactivators, which are products that stimulate new tissue growth. Although there are many types of injectable fillers, the most commonly used have been collagen and fat, which

Table 5–1 Current FDA-Approved Injectable Materials	
Brand Name	**Made From**
Zyderm and Zyplast	**Bovine** collagen
Cosmoderm and Cosmoplast	Bioengineered human collagen
Cymetra	**Cadaver**-derived tissue
Fascian	Cadaver-derived tissue
Radiesse	Calcium hydroxylapatite crystals
Sculptra	Polylactic acid
Restylane	NASHA (nonanimal stabilized hyaluronic acid gel)
Hylaform, Hylaform Plus	Animal-derived hyaluronic acid gel

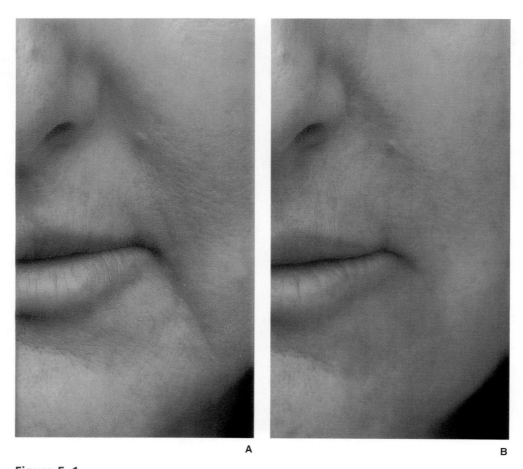

A   B

Figure 5–1

A, Prominent oral commissures. B, Same patient after injection with hylaform. Reprinted with permission from Inamed Aesthetics.

will be discussed in this chapter. Some new fillers, **FDA**-approved in 2004, are based on *hyaluronic acid gel* and are fast becoming as widely used as **collagen** (Figure 5–1).

The results from injectable fillers are usually not permanent; the body eventually metabolizes the substances. However, some materials such as silicone or *Artecoll* (another type of filler that has not yet been approved in the United States) can create a correction that is *permanent*. Because most products last several months rather than years, patients must be prepared to have possible touch-up injections a few times a year.

Body fat makes excellent injectable filler because it is readily available and nonallergenic. However, it is a thick material and cannot be used to fill fine lines. Therefore, it is most often used as contour filler for cheeks, lips, and nasolabial folds.

Injectables are not the only treatment options for facial wrinkles. The wrinkles that form around the eyes or mouth are often treated with resurfacing techniques such as lasers, dermabrasion, or chemical peels. Injectable fillers may be used alone or in conjunction with resurfacing procedures and/or a face-lift.

INDICATIONS

Collagen

Collagen injections are most useful in the treatment of frown lines, "crow's feet," nasolabial folds (Figure 5–2), smoker's lines (Figure 5–3) around the mouth, and lip augmentation. Collagen is also often used to eliminate or reduce scarring from acne and other scars by plumping the depressed scars (Figure 5–4).

Fat

Fat injections are most often used to fill in "sunken" cheeks or smile lines between the nose and mouth, to enhance the lips, to correct scars or indentations, and to minimize forehead wrinkles. Like collagen, fat injections are not permanent and may require a maintenance program. In addition, unlike collagen, which comes readily available in a prepackaged syringe, fat transfer injections require a separate

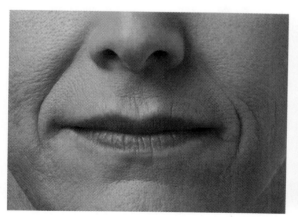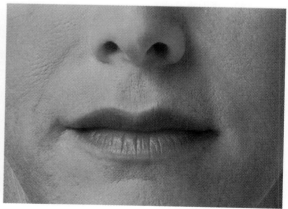

A   B

Figure 5–2

A, Nasolabial lines. B, Same patient after injection with cosmoplast. Reprinted with permission from Inamed Aesthetics.

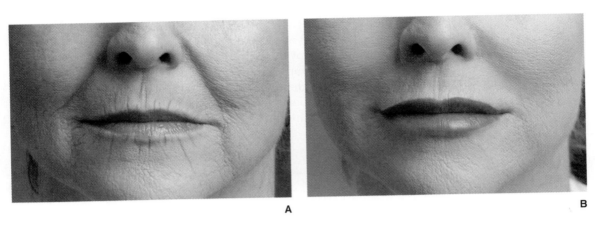

Figure 5–3

A, Smoker's lines. B, Same patient after injection with cosmoderm. Reprinted with permission from Inamed Aesthetics.

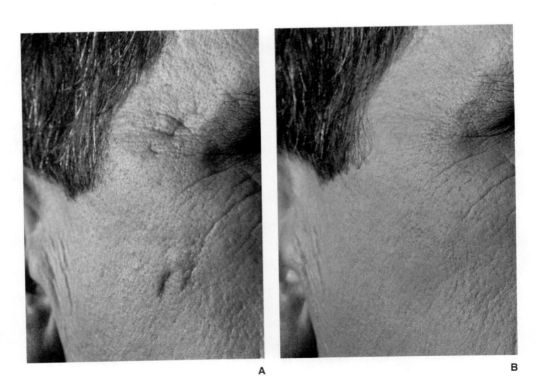

Figure 5–4

A, Deep acne scarring. B, Same patient after injection with cosmoderm. Reprinted with permission from Inamed Aesthetics.

procedure where the fat is first removed from another area of the patient's body.

MECHANISM OF ACTION AND TARGET TISSUES

Collagen

Injectable collagen is purified from bovine (cow) collagen to resemble human collagen. It comes in different **viscosities** to meet each patient's needs. Some trade names include **Zyderm** and **Zyplast**. In addition, a new form of bioengineered human-derived collagen is available under the name **cosmoderm** and **cosmoplast**. This material is identical to the collagen in our own bodies and, thus, has no allergic potential.

Collagen is the major component of the extra-cellular matrix of a variety of connective tissues. In the skin, collagen is the major support matrix and accounts for approximately 80 percent of the total dry weight of the dermis. Time, gravity, sun exposure, and repetitive facial muscle movement are some factors that cause the underlying tissues to break down, leaving laugh lines, smile lines, crow's feet, and other facial creases. Injectable collagen essentially replaces the natural collagen that the skin loses over time and plumps up these wrinkles and facial creases, whereas *injected fat* serves simply to plump up deep wrinkles and depressions (Figure 5–5). Fat inflates the entire area and stretches the skin smoother, whereas collagen only fills in the specific wrinkle or scar.

Figure 5–5

A, Cross-section of wrinkle. B, Cross-section of wrinkle after injection with filler.

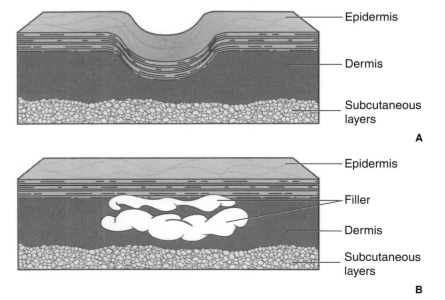

Autologous Fat Injections

Body fat makes excellent soft-tissue filler material. It is transferred from one part of the body to another to recontour the face; diminish frown lines, crow's feet, and nasolabial folds (smile lines); and provide definition to areas like the cheeks and chin. It can also be used to fill out depressed scarred areas on any part of the body. Fat injection is not permanent and may require an effective maintenance program.

A *fat-injection* procedure is known as **autologous fat** transplantation or microlipoinjection. It involves extracting fat cells from the patient's abdomen, thighs, buttocks, or elsewhere and reinjecting them beneath the facial skin or other parts of the body. Because fat is a thicker substance than collagen, it is injected with a larger needle. Therefore, patients having fat injections commonly have more bruising and swelling than patients undergoing collagen injections.

PREPROCEDURE CONSIDERATIONS

Collagen injections are generally off limits for pregnant women, individuals who are allergic to beef or bovine products (this is only true for the use of bovine collagen products), patients who suffer from autoimmune diseases, and those who are allergic to lidocaine because the anesthetic agent lidocaine is mixed with the collagen in the syringe.

Cosmoderm/cosmoplast are bioengineered *human* collagen and have no allergic potential, whereas Zyderm/Zyplast are **bovine derived** and have a small but possible allergic rate in two to three percent of the population. To help determine whether the patient is allergic to the *bovine-derived* collagen, the physician will perform one to two allergy skin tests about a month before the procedure. Any sign of redness, itching, swelling, or other unusual occurrences at the test site should be reported to the treating physician because they signal a potential allergy to the material.

Anesthesia
Collagen

Additional anesthetic is usually not used because the anesthetic agent lidocaine is mixed in with collagen. However, for patients who are especially sensitive to pain, a topical anesthetic or ice packs can be used. Patients may elect to have an injected local anesthetic or sedation, but this is exceedingly rare.

Fat

Before the procedure, both the donor and recipient sites are numbed with **local anesthesia**. Sedation can be used as well.

PROCEDURE/TECHNIQUES

When done as the sole procedure, fillers are usually administered in a physician's office-based facility.

Collagen

Treatment with collagen can begin after a skin test rules out a potential allergy to the substance. This is necessary with bovine collagen but not with human collagen-derived *cosmoderm* or *cosmoplast.* After double skin testing is performed, the test site should be watched carefully for four to six weeks. If the test site remains unreactive, the collagen can then be injected in the face at several points along the treatment site using a fine needle. Depending on the length and depth of the wrinkle, multiple injections are usually needed.

Fat

The donor and recipient sites are prepped and draped and then treated with a local anesthesia. The fat is harvested using a syringe with a large-bore needle or a liposuction **cannula**. The fat is then processed to remove excess fluids and reinjected with another needle in multiple thin strands in the desired area. "Overfilling" is necessary due to fat absorption in the weeks after treatment. For longest-lasting effect, patients generally receive three to four treatments over a six-month period.

When fat is used to fill sunken cheeks or to correct areas on the face other than lines, this overcorrection of newly injected fat may temporarily make the face appear abnormally puffed out or swollen.

Autologous fat is natural and nonallergenic and under normal circumstances cannot be rejected or create an allergic reaction. As a result, no pretesting is required.

Collagen injection can take 15 minutes to perform. However, fat injection usually takes longer because the fat has to be harvested and prepared before it is reinjected.

DRESSINGS AND WOUND CARE

Because the injection is done with needles, dressings are not always required. Collagen injections use small bore needles, so no bandage is needed. However, with fat injections a larger needle is used and some physicians may apply an adhesive bandage over the injection site.

Sutures

Sutures are not usually required after injecting fillers.

Bathing and Hair Care

Bathing and hair care can usually resume immediately after the procedure.

Makeup

After receiving collagen injections, most patients can immediately wear makeup. With more invasive injections like fat, it may be preferable to wait 24 hours for the skin to calm down before applying makeup. Avoiding sunlight and heavy exercise for 24 hours after any type of injections also appears to help reduce any swelling or redness.

Sun Protection

If patients must be outdoors for prolonged periods of time, it is recommended that they wear hats and sunscreen lotions with an SPF of 15 or greater.

POSTPROCEDURE SKIN/TISSUE CHANGES

In some individuals, the results may last only a few weeks; in others, the results may be maintained indefinitely. Age, genetic background, skin quality, and lifestyle as well as the injected body site may all play a role in the injected material's "staying power." However, by far the most important determining factor is the injectable material itself.

Collagen

Immediately after treatment, patients may notice some minor discomfort, stinging, or throbbing in the treated area. Occasionally minor bruising or swelling will occur. Any redness that appears in the injected site usually disappears within 24 hours. However, in some individuals, particularly fair-skinned patients, this redness may persist for about 1 week or more. Tiny scabs may also form over the needle-stick areas; these generally heal quickly.

Because there is saline (salt water) mixed into the collagen syringe, the physician needs to slightly overfill the treated area because the saline will be rapidly absorbed, reducing the amount of "correction" seen with the immediate injection.

Fat

Some swelling, bruising, or redness in both the donor and recipient sites is normal. The severity of these symptoms depends on the size and location of the treated area. However, there is always more swelling, bruising, and tenderness with fat injections than with collagen injections.

The duration of the fat injections varies significantly from patient to patient. Though some patients have reported results lasting a year or more, most patients find that at least half of the injected fullness disappears within three to six months. Therefore, repeated injections may be necessary.

POSTPROCEDURE ACTIVITIES

In general, patients should avoid exercise or other strenuous activities for 24 hours after injections. After that time patients should be able to resume their normal activities.

SOME RISKS AND POSSIBLE COMPLICATIONS

When a qualified physician administers injectable fillers, complications are infrequent and usually minor. The outcome of treatment with injectables is never completely predictable. Risks include:

Collagen

- Allergic reaction is the primary risk of bovine collagen.
- Infection/abscesses.
- Open sores/**ulcers**.
- Skin peeling.
- Scarring and lumpiness over the treated area.

Fat

- Allergic reaction is not a factor for fat because it is harvested from a patient's own body.
- Infection/abscesses.
- Open sores/ulcers.
- Skin peeling.
- Scarring and lumpiness over the treated area.

Chapter 6

Chemical Face Peels

Mark G. Rubin, MD

Chemical peels are a safe and effective way to improve the texture and appearance of the skin. They may also remove precancerous skin growths, soften acne facial scars, and help control acne. Like laser resurfacing, *chemical peeling* can provide a "finishing touch" after a face-lift by improving surface wrinkles and refining the overall texture and appearance of the skin. **Chemical peels** are categorized as light, medium, or deep, depending on the depth of the peel, which in turn is dependent on the chemical solution, its concentration, and the application technique.

INDICATIONS

Light Peels

- Used to smooth and brighten skin—usually performed as part of a series of treatments
- Helps control acne
- Improves uneven pigmentation
- Improves texture of sun-damaged skin
- Can be used on nonfacial areas such as the neck and chest

Medium Peels

- Improves fine wrinkles and moderate sun damage
- Commonly used for pigmentation problems (Figure 6–1)
- Rarely done on neck or other body areas as it may cause scarring

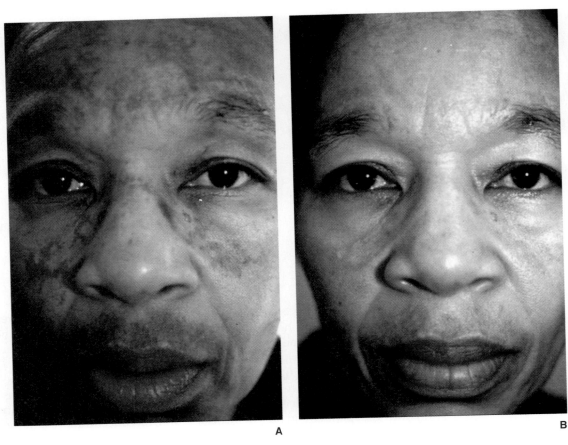

Figure 6–1

A, Woman with melasma. B, Same woman two months after a Jessner's solution face peel. Reprinted with the permission of the American Academy of Dermatology. All rights reserved.

Deep Peels

- Used to treat deep, course wrinkles from sun exposure
- Wrinkling around the lips and chin area
- Age spots, uneven pigmentation, scarring or precancerous growths
- Not recommended for most patients with dark skin, due to its lightening effect
- Should not be used on the neck or other parts of the patient's body

MECHANISM OF ACTION AND TARGET TISSUES

As the reader is well aware, the skin is made up of several layers: the epidermis, the dermis, and the subcutaneous layer. The dermis is

	Epidermis	Dermis	
Table 6–1 Penetration of the Chemicals		*Papillary*	*Reticular*
LIGHT PEELS	Yes	No	No
Alpha Hydroxy Acid (AHA)			
(Glycolic Acid, Lactic Acid)			
Beta Hydroxy Acid (Salicylic Acid)			
Jessner's Solution (Salicylic Acid, Resorcinol and Lactic Acid)			
MEDIUM PEELS	Yes	Yes	No
Trichloroacetic Acid (TCA)			
DEEP PEELS	Yes	Yes	Yes
Phenol Chemical Peels			
Deep–TCA			

made up of two layers: the superficial portion is known as the papillary dermis and the deeper portion is known as the reticular dermis. Both contain collagen and elastin.

Chemical solutions must meet each patient's needs, because the active ingredient and concentration of the chemical will determine what layers will be affected. The stronger the peel, the deeper it will penetrate. Several types of chemicals can be used to exfoliate the damaged outer layers of the epidermis. Other chemicals will penetrate deeper into the dermis to increase the synthesis of collagen and elastin (Table 6–1).

Light Peels

The acids in this group are mild, allowing the gentle exfoliation of the epidermis. Commonly used light peeling agents include *alpha hydroxy acid* (**AHA**), salicylic acid, and **Jessner's solution**. This level of peel will usually not affect the dermis. Light peels will only improve color and texture, not wrinkles and scars.

Medium Peels

The acids in this group are stronger than those used for light peels and weaker than the phenol used in deep peels. *Trichloroacetic acid* (TCA) is the most common peeling agent for medium-depth peels. At 30 to 35 percent concentrations, TCA will penetrate through the epidermis and into the papillary dermis to stimulate collagen synthesis.

Deep Peels

A deep peel is an extreme *one-time* procedure that can produce dramatic, long-lasting results. In many cases improvement is apparent some 20 years after a phenol peel. Phenol (carbolic acid) is the strongest of the chemical peel solutions, causing the deepest skin peel; it penetrates into the *reticular layer* of the dermis, stimulating marked collagen synthesis.

Although high-strength TCA (50 percent or more) can be used for deep chemical peels, it appears to create more scarring than deep peels created with phenol. Therefore deep TCA peeling is rarely done.

For most superficial and medium-depth peels, the skin is pretreated, or "primed" with topical creams, for several weeks before the peel. This is done to stimulate epidermal cell growth, leading to faster healing from the peel, and to thin the dead cell layer (**stratum corneum**). This allows the peel solution to penetrate more evenly and deeply. Although *Retin-A* is the most commonly used topical agent to prime the skin for a peel, if the patient cannot tolerate Retin-A, an AHA cream may be used instead. **Hydroquinone** (a bleaching agent) is often used in conjunction with Retin-A or AHA pretreatment, especially if the patient has blotchy skin areas or pigmentation problems. In most cases this "priming" phase of the peel takes about two weeks. However, in severely damaged, thick skin, this phase can take up to one month.

If a patient is allergic to hydroquinone, which is quite rare, other bleaching agents may be used (e.g., *kojic acid* or *azelaic acid*). However, the latter two are not as effective as hydroquinone.

PREPROCEDURE CONSIDERATIONS

Before a chemical peel, it is important for a patient to inform the physician of any past, unusual scarring tendencies, such as **keloids**, or pertinent history, such as X-rays or radiation to the face, or recurring cold sores (**herpes simplex I**). Birth control pills, pregnancy, or a family history of brownish discoloration on the face may increase the possibility of developing abnormal hyperpigmentation. To reduce this complication, patients at risk for this complication need to have their skin "primed" with bleachers before having their peel performed.

There is a risk of reactivation of cold sores or herpes simplex infection in patients with a history of fever blisters. The deeper the peel, the more common the problem is. The use of prophylactic oral antiviral agents before the peel can help prevent a herpes infection.

Anesthesia

Light Peels

No anesthesia or **sedation** is needed; the patient will feel only a mild tingling or stinging sensation when the solution is applied. This rapidly dissipates within a few minutes.

Medium Peels

During the procedure, most patients experience a hot stinging sensation that may last about 5 to 10 minutes. Although some patients find this level peel quite uncomfortable, the procedure is very brief, so anesthesia is usually not required; however, a light **sedative** may be used to help relax the patient before and during the procedure.

Deep Peels

Phenol peeling is very painful. Patients are usually fully sedated or pretreated with nerve blocks before the application of the phenol. There is usually some discomfort for one to two days postpeel, and some patients will require oral **analgesics**, postpeel.

PROCEDURE/TECHNIQUES

Most chemical peels may be safely performed in a physician's office, office-based surgical facility, or outpatient surgical center. The hair is moved out of the way. For optimal penetration, the skin is cleansed to remove oils, dirt, and traces of soap. Using a sponge, cotton pad, cotton swab, or brush, the solution is applied. Care is taken to avoid getting the solution in the eyes or on the brows and lips (Figure 6–2).

Figure 6–2
Applying chemicals.

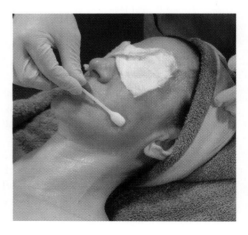

Light Peels

Alpha hydroxy acid (AHA), salicylic acid, or Jessner's solution is applied to the facial skin, a process that usually takes no more than 10 minutes. The depth of these peels, in addition to being dependent on the concentration of the acid, is either dependent on the number of coats of acid applied (Jessner's or salicylic acid peels), or how long the acid is in contact with the skin. With AHA no ointment or **occlusive mask** is required. Depending on the strength of the peel, they are repeated every few weeks, until the desired effect is achieved. The superficial AHA is often called the "lunch hour" peel because it can be done quickly and there is no downtime.

Medium Peels

In most cases, only 1 application is needed; however, to achieve the desired results, 2 or more TCA applications may be needed over a span of several months. If another peel is performed, there must be enough time allotted between the peels to allow the skin to heal completely from the first peel. Medium TCA peels may be repeated as often as 6 to 8 weeks. TCA peeling is a short and relatively safe procedure. A full-face TCA peel can be done in approximately 10 to 15 minutes. After the application of the TCA, the physician may apply an ointment over the treated area. TCA can be used in many concentrations, but it is most commonly used for medium-depth peeling in concentrations of 30 to 35 percent.

Deep Peels

Phenol application may pose a risk for patients due to its cardiac toxicity, thus **EKG** monitoring is advised during the procedure and in the recovery room.

The phenol solution is slowly applied to the skin in sections, allowing the solution to flush through the system before the next area is treated. Approximately one hour later, petroleum jelly is applied to cover the protective crust, which will develop rapidly over the treated area. In cases of severe wrinkling, an **occlusive mask**, which is composed of waterproof strips of adhesive tape, may be applied to cover the patient's face, with openings for the eyes and mouth. It stays in place for one to two days. The mask increases the penetration of the peel, increasing its efficacy.

Some physicians will apply **thymol iodine** powder to the skin after the peel, which creates a heavy crust. Other physicians prefer to apply an ointment to keep the skin moist and prevent the formation of a crust.

Full-face phenol peels take approximately one to two hours, but small-area phenol peels, such as on the upper lip or chin, may take about 10 to 15 minutes.

DRESSINGS AND WOUND CARE

Light Peels

No dressings or ointments are required. Normal bathing and gentle cleansing of the face can resume the morning after the procedure. However, because there is increased dryness and flaking, additional use of moisturizers is normally required. Also, topical products containing active agents such as retinoids, vitamin C, AHAs and exfoliants should not be used during the healing phase of these peels because the skin is more sensitive during this time.

Medium Peels

Swelling, redness, and severe drying of the skin is normal. About 2 to 3 days after the application of the TCA peel, a dark, shiny layer of dead skin forms, which serves to protect the underlying new skin (Figure 6–3). In most cases, over the course of 5 to 7 days this brown layer falls off on its own. During this healing phase, physicians will usually instruct patients to apply an ointment, cream, or heavy moisturizer to their skin and to ignore the urge to remove the peeling skin.

Deep Peels

If an occlusive mask (made of tape) was applied, it is usually removed in 1 to 2 days. Swelling and crusting of the skin is normal for approximately 10 days postprocedure. As previously mentioned, some physicians may instruct patients to apply an ointment to their healing skin, rather than to allow a crust to form.

Sutures

No sutures.

Bathing and Hair Care

With light peels, the face can be gently washed starting later that day. Normal bathing and gentle cleansing of the face can resume the morning after a light face peel. With medium and deep chemical peels, very gentle rinsing of the skin can be performed within 24 hours. No scrubbing of

Figure 6–3

Dark, shiny layer post-TCA peel. Photo provided by Mark G. Rubin, MD.

the face is allowed until the epidermis is completely healed (i.e., no oozing or draining). The face should be blotted with a fresh towel, not rubbed. If the hair is being shampooed, care should be taken to rinse out the shampoo backward away from the face. Accidentally getting shampoo on the healing face can create some stinging and burning but rarely causes a more significant problem.

Makeup

Makeup can be applied shortly after the skin has regained its integrity (i.e., no oozing or draining). This can range from days up to two weeks, depending on the strength and depth of the chemical peel. If the patient has or develops a reaction to makeup after the peel, the physician may recommend nonallergenic makeup and the use of a topical anti-inflammatory (**cortisone**) cream.

Sun Protection

Because all level peels can at least temporarily damage the pigmentation production of the skin, *all patients are advised to avoid sun exposure for several months* after their peel treatment to protect the newly formed layers of skin. Patients need to wear a broad-spectrum sunscreen daily (SPF 15 or greater). In general, fanatical avoidance of the sun helps decrease the risk of pigmentation abnormalities. Failure to protect the skin from the sun can result in uneven skin pigmentation and blotching.

Because most phenol peel (deep peel) patients have some permanent lightening of their skin, they lose their ability to tan. Thus, these patients will require *lifelong* sun protection (at least SPF 15) and a wide-brimmed hat when outdoors.

POSTPROCEDURE SKIN/TISSUE CHANGES

Light Peels

AHA peels may cause stinging, redness, irritation, flaking, and scaling. Improvements from AHA peels may be very subtle at first, with a healthier glow to the skin; after several treatments, patients should also notice a smoother texture. Patients who experience any increase in redness, pain, or crusting with a light- or medium-depth peel in the days after surgery should notify their physician immediately.

Medium Peels

About one day after the peel, a brown shiny layer of dead skin forms. Patients may experience some minor swelling, which usually subsides within the first day or two. Patients are instructed not to pick at their old skin because it could result in infections or scarring. In six to eight days after the peel, new skin is exposed that is pink, more evenly pigmented, and has a smoother texture. It will take about a week for all the redness to vanish. Patients may be instructed to apply an ointment, cream, or moisturizer after cleaning their skin. Most physicians like to keep the skin moist as it heals.

Although TCA is milder than phenol, it may also produce some unintended color changes in the skin. In darker-skinned patients, temporary darkening of the skin (postinflammatory **hyperpigmentation**) can occur. This is a self-limited response that will gradually fade over time but can be improved rapidly with the use of topical bleaching agents.

In a very small percentage of patients, persistent lightening (**hypopigmentation**) of the skin may occur. Hypopigmentation is commonly seen with phenol peeling but fortunately is fairly uncommon with medium-depth TCA peeling. Patients who experience any increase in redness, pain, or crusting with a light- or medium-depth peel in the days after surgery should notify their physician immediately.

The results of a TCA peel are usually not as long-lasting as those of phenol peel. However, with good maintenance skin care, the results of a medium-depth peel should last for several years.

Deep Peels

Deep peeling normally creates swelling and blisters that may break, crust, flake, turn brown, and peel off over a period of 7 to 14 days or longer. The swelling may be severe enough that the patient's eyes may be temporarily swollen shut. While the skin is healing, the patient may experience itching, burning, or tingling, which can be minimized with medications and/or cold compresses. In about 7 to 10 days postpeel, the new skin is exposed as the crust peels off. The new skin is usually bright red (similar to a bad sunburn), gradually turning to a lighter pink. Skin redness that persists after the initial healing phase will usually fade in about 4 weeks.

After an extended recovery period, patients who have undergone a deep phenol peel should have markedly fewer wrinkles, scars, and blemishes and much improved skin tone. However, due to the depth of the tissue change, permanent skin lightening and lines of demarcation may occur.

With *deep phenol peels,* the skin tightens and wrinkles appear diminished, but the pores may appear larger. This appears to be related to the tightening of the skin, which stretches the skin and makes the pores appear larger. This change in pore size is usually an *irreversible* problem.

Scars

Although very low, there is a risk of scarring after chemical peels. In general, the deeper the peel, the greater the chance for scarring. Also if the patient picks at his or her skin or develops an infection, the risk of scarring increases dramatically. If scarring occurs, it can usually be treated, and improved, but cannot be entirely eliminated.

POSTPROCEDURE ACTIVITIES

Light Peels

There is no downtime; thus, the name **lunch time peel**.

Medium Peels

After about 10 days, patients should be ready to resume their daily activities. Although patients with a TCA peel usually return to their normal activities in about a week to 10 days, they should refrain from strenuous activities for 2 to 3 weeks to reduce redness and any irritation from sweating. The recovery from a TCA peel is longer than a light peel but usually shorter than with a phenol peel.

Deep Peels

Usually, patients wait about two weeks to get back to most of their normal activities, including work. Due to the swelling during the first few days postpeel, the physician often recommends a soft diet, avoidance of extremes in temperature, and any activity that would cause stress to healing skin. These patients will have some significant redness for at least several weeks postpeel. Therefore they will need to wear some type of *camouflage makeup* before returning to their normal social and business activities.

SOME RISKS AND POSSIBLE COMPLICATIONS

The results from chemical peels will depend on the chemical solution, its application, the patient's skin type, and the patient's coloring. The deeper the peel procedure, the more intense each aspect of the patient's recovery will be, but the more profound the improvement in wrinkles and scars will be as well.

Like all surgery, chemical peels involve some level of risk. However, when performed by, or under the direction of, an experienced physician, they are normally safe procedures. It is imperative that patients follow the preoperative and postoperative instructions of their physician to the letter to avoid complications. Possible risks include:

- Although extremely rare, there is always the risk of infection.
- Scarring and uneven skin pigmentation, although infrequent, are possible.
- Reactivation of cold sores or herpes simplex infection is possible.

A face cream containing low-concentration alpha hydroxy acid, used as part of a daily skin-care regimen, and applied at least once or twice a day at home, is usually sufficient to accomplish the desired goal. Retin-A or a bleaching agent is occasionally added to the at-home treatment schedule. After several weeks of at-home use, the physician will reevaluate the patient's skin and adjust accordingly.

- Failure to protect the skin from the sun can result in uneven skin pigmentation and blotching.
- Phenol may pose a special risk for patients, especially those with a history of heart disease.
- With deep phenol peels, the pores may appear larger, which is usually irreversible.

Chapter 7

Dermabrasion

Microdermabrasion uses a hand-held device that forcibly propels a stream of tiny, sterile micronized aluminum oxide crystals onto the skin surface. It is suggested that the resulting gentle abrasion stimulates the production of new skin cells and collagen, which gives the skin a fresh, healthy glow. It is also claimed to reduce age spots, fine wrinkles, and some acne scars. No anesthesia is required and there are virtually no side effects. There is practically no recovery or downtime, and normal activities can be resumed immediately. Although the procedure generally takes less than one hour to perform, multiple maintenance treatments are required, usually spaced two to three weeks apart.

In as much as these devices have been classified as cosmetic rather than medical, they are not subject to the rigors of the FDA.

Dermabrasion is a nonthermal resurfacing procedure that, as its name implies, abrades layers of skin through the controlled removal of the epidermis and *upper* dermis. Dermabrasion stimulates new, healthier-appearing skin to replace and smooth damaged skin with sharp edges or surface irregularities, giving the skin a smoother appearance.

It was first used more than 100 years ago to smooth out surface irregularities of the facial skin resulting from acne, chicken pox, and accidents. However, for the most part, chemical peels and laser skin resurfacing are replacing dermabrasion.

INDICATIONS

Dermabrasion is most often used to treat acne scarring, particularly depressed scars that give the skin a crater-like appearance (Figure 7–1). It is also used on wrinkles around eyes, cheeks, and mouth (smoker's lines), as well as sun-induced brown "liver spots." In addition, dermabrasion is used for treating **rhinophyma**, which occurs when sebaceous glands enlarge, resulting in a bulbous and irregular, red nose. Dermabrasion sculpts the nose down to a more normal shape and appearance. It is also sometimes used to remove precancerous growths called **keratosis**.

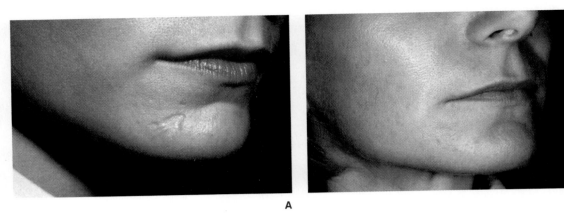

Figure 7–1

A, Patient with depressed scar on chin. B, Same patient several years after dermabrasion. Reprinted with the permission of the American Academy of Dermatology. All rights reserved.

MECHANISM OF ACTION AND TARGET TISSUES

Dermabrasion is performed with an abrasive wheel or brush that is attached to a high-speed rotary instrument. The mechanical sanding destroys the upper layer of the skin much like that caused by chemical peels, superficial thermal burns, the removal of a split-thickness skin graft, or laser.

The primarily **histological** basis for new epithelial cells after dermabrasion rests on the capacity of the skin to regenerate a new epithelial layer from hair shafts that are part of skin appendages known as **pilosebaceous units** (Figure 7–2). Epithelial cell outgrowth from the shaft of the hair follicles combines with marginal epithelialization from the edges of the wound to completely cover the raw skin surface in five to seven days. At the same time, new collagen formation occurs with fibroblast proliferation and new capillary formation.

PREPROCEDURE CONSIDERATIONS

Although older people heal more slowly, more important factors are the skin type, coloring, and medical history. For example, dark complexions may become permanently discolored or blotchy after dermabrasion. Freckles may disappear in the treated area.

> A **split-thickness skin graft** (STSG) contains all of the epidermis and some of the dermis. The pilosebaceous units in the donor site retain the ability to resurface the donor site with new epithelial cells. Split-thickness skin grafts are harvested with dermatomes. STSGs are commonly used to repair third-degree burns. A **full-thickness skin graft** (FTSG) contains epidermis and ALL of the dermis. The donor site must be closed by suturing because there is no pilosebaceous units left to regenerate the epidermis. FTSGs are sometimes used to repair full tissue defects on the face.

Figure 7–2

Pilosebaceous unit.

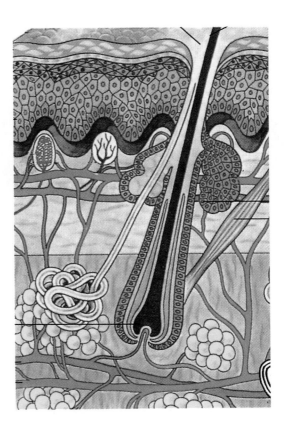

In **_dermaplaning_,** the surgeon uses a hand-held instrument called a dermatome, the same surgical instrument used to harvest split-thickness skin grafts. Resembling an electric razor, the dermatome has an oscillating blade that moves back and forth to evenly "shave" off the surface layers of skin that surround the craters or other facial defects. Dermaplaning can be used to treat deep acne scars on the cheeks and forehead. Both dermabrasion and dermaplaning can be performed on small areas of skin or on the entire face.

Most physicians will not perform dermabrasion with active acne because of a greater risk of infection. Other contraindications may include: prior radiation treatments, a bad skin burn, and patients on **Accutane**. Dermabrasion can also activate latent herpes simplex infections.

Although patients may go home after dermabrasion, they should have someone drive them home, as well as arrange for someone to help out around the house for a few days.

Anesthesia

Dermabrasion may be performed under local anesthesia with a sedative. The patient will be awake but relaxed and will feel minimal discomfort. Occasionally, a topical anesthetic is used along with or instead of local anesthesia. In severe cases, the physician may prefer to use general anesthesia.

Figure 7–3

Dermabrasion in progress.

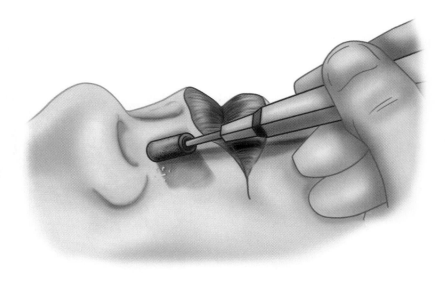

PROCEDURE/TECHNIQUES

Dermabrasion can be performed in the physician's office or in an outpatient surgical facility. The area is thoroughly cleansed with an **antiseptic cleanser**. Then, using a hand-held, high-speed rotating sanding wheel or brush, the affected area is essentially "sanded down" through the epidermis and into the dermis of the skin (Figure 7–3).

DRESSINGS AND WOUND CARE

After dermabrasion, the treated skin will weep until the surface regenerates a new epidermis—usually for about one week. During this period, the wound must be kept moist and treated with care.

Typically, the first dressing change is done in the physician's office within the first 24 hours. Then, every other day for approximately 7 to 8 days or until the skin surface is completely reepithelialized. Soothing ointment and/or dressings keep the skin moist until the new skin layer reforms. As it begins to heal, a scab or crust will form over the treated area. This will fall off as a new layer of tight, pink skin forms underneath. If a dressing is used and stuck to the wound, it should NOT be forcibly pulled from the wound. Doing so may contribute to scarring. To minimize the likelihood of scab formation and help speed the skin's recovery, the wound should be cleaned with cotton balls soaked with the prescribed cleansing solution and blotted dry before applying the ointment—if so prescribed.

A stuck dressing should be soaked with saline solution to loosen it before removal.

Medications may be prescribed to alleviate any discomfort the patient may have, but most people do not experience severe pain. A specialized preoperative and postoperative skin care plan may be recommended to maximize improvement and protect the resurfaced skin.

Sutures

Sutures are not used for dermabrasion or dermaplaning.

Bathing and Hair Care

Most physicians allow patients to resume bathing one to three days postoperative. Patients should be especially gentle with the face, because the skin will be tender. The face should be washed gently every day, followed by the application of a thin layer of the prescribed ointment. Shampooing, hair care, and gentle brushing can resume as early as the third postoperative day. Men should delay shaving for a while, then only with an electric razor until cleared by their physician to resume using the razor. Steam baths and saunas should be avoided for several months or until cleared by the surgeon.

Makeup

Makeup can be applied shortly after the skin has healed. This can range from five to seven days. If the patient has, or develops, a reaction to makeup after the dermabrasion, the physician may recommend nonallergenic makeup and the use of a topical anti-inflammatory (cortisone) cream.

Sun Protection

It is important to avoid unprotected, direct sun exposure for several months after dermabrasion, or until the skin color has returned to normal, usually 6 to 12 months. If patients must be outdoors for prolonged periods of time, it is recommended that they wear hats and sunscreen lotions with an SPF of 15 or greater.

Immediately after the procedure, the skin will be red and swollen. Sometimes eating and talking may be affected. The swelling will begin to subside in a few days to a week. During this time, tenderness or a sunburn sensation is expected. In addition, the patient may feel some tingling, burning, or aching. Most of this pain can be controlled with oral analgesics.

The treated area may remain bright pink for several weeks. The treated skin may itch as new skin starts to grow, but an ointment can usually make the patient more comfortable.

Most patients will heal within one to two weeks, and most patients will notice a significant improvement in their skin quality and appearance. However, the subtle signs of continuing improvement will usually occur for 6 to 12 months.

Change in skin pigmentation is the most common side effect. Permanent darkening of the skin, usually caused by exposure to the sun in the days or months after surgery, may occur in some patients. Increased pigmentation can be treated with bleaching creams, but decreased pigmentation may be permanent. On the other hand, in some patients the treated skin may remain blotchy in appearance.

When the new skin is fully repigmented, the color should closely match the surrounding skin, making the procedure virtually undetectable.

Milia (tiny whiteheads) are pinpoint areas of white sebum that often appear postoperatively due to a temporary blockage of ductal orifices during reepithelialization of the treated skin (Figure 7–4). With time, these usually disappear. If not, they may require the use of an

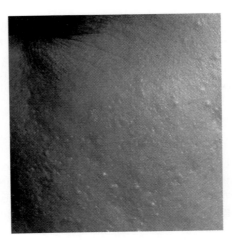

Figure 7–4
Milia.

abrasive pad or soapy facecloth. Occasionally, milia may need to be unroofed to express the material.

Patients may also develop *enlarged skin pores,* which usually shrink to near normal size once the swelling has subsided.

Scars

Some people may develop slightly thickened skin, **hypertrophic scars,** or **keloids** after dermabrasion.

POSTPROCEDURE ACTIVITIES

Patients may be instructed to keep their head elevated for the first several days postoperative. Some patients are instructed to apply cooling packs over the dressings.

Most patients can resume their normal activities in 7 to 10 days, and they can usually expect to be back at work in about 2 weeks. Patients may be advised to avoid any activity that could expose the face to injury for at least 2 weeks. Contact sports should be avoided for 4 to 6 weeks. Swimmers should keep their face out of chlorinated water or the ocean until cleared by their physician. It will be at least 3 to 4 weeks before patients can drink alcohol without experiencing a flush of redness.

SOME RISKS AND POSSIBLE COMPLICATIONS

As with any surgery, dermabrasion involves some level of risk; although complications with this type of surgery are rare, they can and do occur. Most risks, however, can be minimized when performed by a properly trained and experienced physician. Possible risks include:

- Infection
- Scarring
- Change in skin pigmentation
- Tiny whiteheads (milia)
- Temporary enlargement of skin pores

Chapter 8

Lasers in Aesthetic Medicine

■ Judith E. Crowell, MD

> **LASER** is an acronym that stands for **l**ight **a**mplification by **s**timulated **e**mission of **r**adiation.

Due to improved technology, relative ease of use, and low incidence of posttreatment complications, the demand for laser surgery in *aesthetic medicine* has increased dramatically over the past 25 years.

A variety of lasers are used to treat assorted conditions. Many procedures can be performed with different lasers, and no single laser can treat all conditions. As such, this chapter will cover some representative lasers and laser treatments commonly used in *aesthetic medicine*.

INDICATIONS

Lasers enjoy wide applications in *aesthetic medicine,* including, but not limited to:

- Skin resurfacing
- Removal of some skin growths
- Treatment of skin photoaging
- Spider veins (Figure 8–1)
- Treatment of rosacea (Figure 8–2)
- Treatment of rhinophyma (Figure 8–3)
- Treatment of pigmented lesions (Figure 8–4)
- Hair removal (Figure 8–5)
- Tattoo removal (Figures 8–6 and 8–7)

Skin resurfacing is by far one of the most popular applications. It resurfaces and tightens loose facial skin and it is a popular alternative to traditional nonsurgical methods for rejuvenation of the face (e.g., dermabrasion and deep chemical peels).

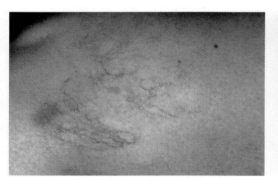 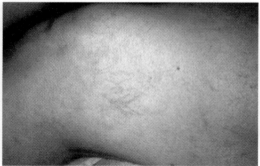

Figure 8–1 A B

A, Spider vein. B, Spider vein after laser treatment. Reprinted with the permission of the American Academy of Dermatology. All rights reserved.

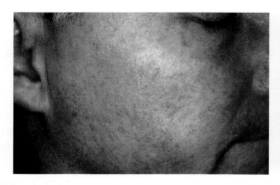 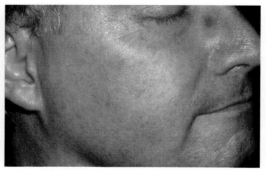

Figure 8–2 A B

A, Rosacea. B, Rosacea after laser treatment. Reprinted with the permission of the American Academy of Dermatology. All rights reserved.

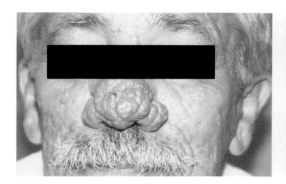 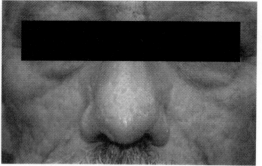

Figure 8–3 A B

A, Rhinophyma. B, Rhinophyma after laser treatment. Photos provided by Judith Crowell, MD.

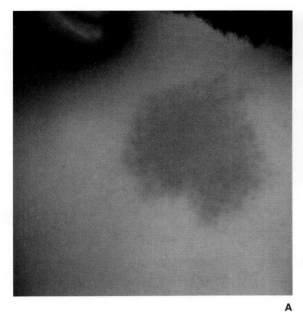

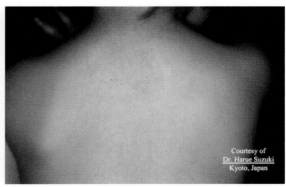

Figure 8–4

A, Pigmented lesion of back. B, Pigmented lesion of back after laser treatment. Photo courtesy of HOYA ConBio on behalf of Dr. Harue Suzuki, Kyoto, Japan.

A

B

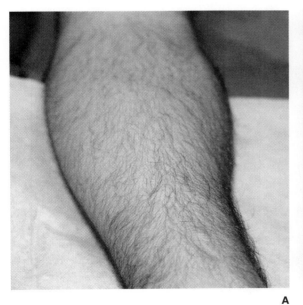

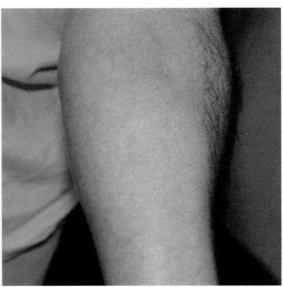

A

B

Figure 8–5

A, Hair removal. B, Hair removal after laser treatment. Photo courtesy of HOYA ConBio on behalf of David Sire, MD, Fullerton, California.

 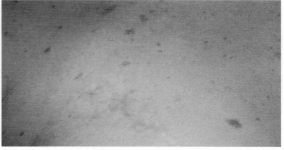

A   B

Figure 8–6

A, Tattoo "rose on breast." B, Tattoo "rose on breast" after laser treatment. Photo courtesy of HOYA ConBio on behalf of David H. McDaniel, MD, Laser Center of Virginia.

A   B

Figure 8–7

A, Tattoo "multicolored bird." B, Tattoo "multicolored bird" after laser treatment. Photo courtesy of HOYA ConBio on behalf of Suzanne Kilmer, MD and R. Rox Anderson, MD, Massachusetts General Hospital.

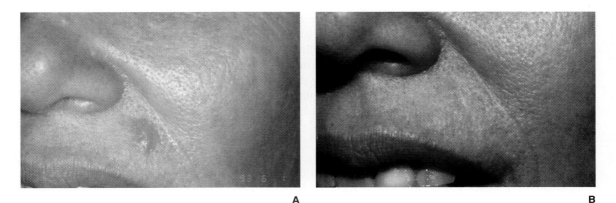

A B

Figure 8–8

A, Scar on upper lip. B, Scar on upper lip after laser treatment. Reprinted with the permission of the American Academy of Dermatology. All rights reserved.

Laser skin resurfacing is also applied in conjunction with other *aesthetic medical* procedures such as blepharoplasty (eyelid surgery), liposuction of the face and neck, face-lift, collagen, facial implants, and botulinum toxin. Some skin growths that can be treated with laser include viral warts, **actinic keratosis**, **seborrheic keratosis**, and *scars* (Figure 8–8).

MECHANISM OF ACTION AND TARGET TISSUES

All lasers work by selective **photothermolysis**. It is selective because each laser's beam is best absorbed by a certain target in the skin. For instance, for the destruction of blood vessels, the pulse dye laser targets hemoglobin in the red blood cells. The term *photo* refers to the column of *light* made up of one or more wavelength(s) produced by each laser. The term *thermo* is used because the laser's light energy is converted into *heat,* which destroys the target tissue.

The pulse dye laser emits a column of yellow light at a specific wavelength that is absorbed by **hemoglobin** within the red blood cells and converted to heat, which disrupts the wall of the blood vessel and is only somewhat absorbed by pigment in the skin. To limit damage to surrounding healthy tissue, a laser's intensity (energy) and pulse duration (the time the skin is exposed to the laser's beam) must be adjustable. This is important because the stronger the intensity and the longer the pulse duration, the greater the area of damage to the surrounding tissue. For a laser to be effective, it needs to selectively destroy the target with minimal or no harm to the surrounding tissue.

Three components are required to produce a laser beam: an energy source, an active medium (either solid, gas, or liquid), and a feedback mechanism (produced with the use of mirror). The atoms located in the **active medium** become "excited" by the *energy source,* resulting in the production of photons (light), which bounce back and forth off the *feedback mechanism* of mirrors, causing a buildup in the intensity of the resulting laser beam. The mirror at one end of the laser tube is semitransparent, allowing some of the photons to pass through the laser beam. This beam is a form of nonionizing radiation with the unique ability to produce monochromatic light (one color) or several (tunable) pure colors.

As with all surgery, the laser has its limitations. The results are technique-sensitive and entail an artistic component on the part of the physician or technician. Aftereffects and recovery times vary with different laser procedures and beam characteristics and, depending on the condition being treated, more than one treatment session may be required. The optimal time period between treatments depends on the type of laser treatment.

Hair Removal

In laser *hair removal* the beam of "invisible light" passes through the skin to the roots of hair follicles, where it is transformed into heat, which disables the hair follicles and reduces their ability to regrow new hair. A marked reduction in hair growth is achieved in three to six visits, depending on the treatment site. After several months, dormant hairs start to regrow and another treatment will be needed. Eventually the thick dark hairs will be drastically reduced.

Skin Resurfacing with Ablative Lasers

There are many lasers for skin resurfacing; they are all **ablative lasers**. Ablative lasers are best at removing the signs of **photoaging**, age spots, superficial blood vessels, and wrinkles; the carbon dioxide (CO_2) laser is the gold standard for skin resurfacing. In the dermis, thermal injury stimulates collagen formation and remodeling, resulting in skin tightening and improvement of wrinkles (Figure 8–9). As

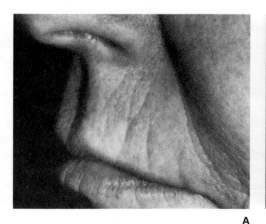 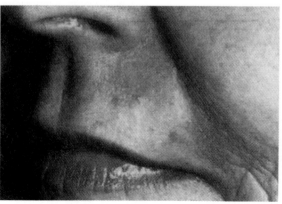

A   B

Figure 8–9

A, Smoker's lines, upper lip. B, Smoker's lines, upper lip after CO_2 laser treatment. Reprinted with permission from *The American Journal of Cosmetic Surgery.*

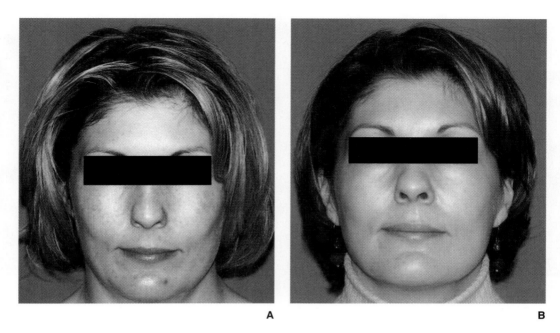

Figure 8–10

A, Blotchy face. B, Same patient after resurfacing with ablative laser. Photo courtesy of HOYA ConBio on behalf of Bryan Rubach, MD, Aurora, Illinois.

with all ablative lasers, the surface of the skin is removed and, with it, the dark blemishes (Figure 8–10) and superficial blood vessels.

The target of the CO_2 laser beam is the water in the cells of the skin. Uptake of the CO_2 laser's energy causes vaporization of the surface cells and **denaturing** of collagen in the dermis, essentially mimicking a burn injury. As a result, the treated skin becomes an open wound until new epithelial cells grow to cover the dermis, a process called reepithelialization.

After the skin reepithelializes, usually within the first 7 to 10 days, there will be a dramatic and immediate improvement in the texture and appearance of the treated skin. However, the color will be that of significant sunburn. Much of this early improvement is due to swelling, which resolves over the next three months. After the third month, when the swelling has resolved, the patient may become concerned as more wrinkles return to the face. However, healing is not complete. The effect of collagen formation and remodeling is not visible until the fourth month; therefore, some of the initial improvement is lost before the more permanent results are seen. It may take up to

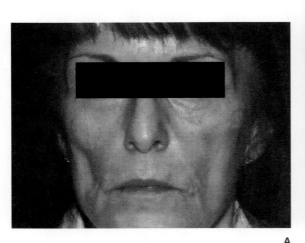 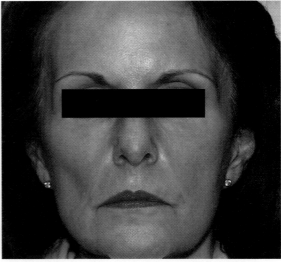

A   B

Figure 8–11

A, Aging face. B, Aging face resurfacing with nonablative laser. Photos courtesy of Judith Crowell, MD.

1 year for the final results of laser skin resurfacing to be achieved. Although, results will be long-lasting, like face-lifts, they are not permanent. Laser skin resurfacing may need to be repeated in 5 to 10 years.

Treating Wrinkles and Scarring with Nonablative Lasers

Nonablative lasers leave the surface of the skin intact, therefore doing nothing to improve the unevenness of the skin's tone and/or color. These lasers are primarily used to treat fine to moderate wrinkles, acne scars, and active acne.

In contrast with ablative lasers, nonablative lasers bypass the epidermis to treat the dermis directly, leaving the surface of the skin intact (Figure 8–11). Four to six treatments are usually necessary because the results from nonablative techniques are generally less than those seen after ablative laser treatments.

PREPROCEDURE CONSIDERATIONS

Before commencing the use of any laser, the physician or technician must have a full understanding of the possible unwanted side effects and how to best avoid them. The preparation will depend on the type of laser used, as well as the area to be treated. Appropriate creams and medications may be recommended to optimize results and protect the treated skin.

Laser procedures with the greatest risk will require the most preoperative work-up. Therefore ablative lasers will require a routine history and physical. This includes inquiry about the patient's history of herpes infections, *cold sores*, fever blisters, sun sensitivity, sun exposure, facial hyperpigmentation, drug use, smoking habits, problems with wound healing, and prior cosmetic procedures (particularly those of the face and neck). The thermal injury delivered to the dermis by ablative, and even nonablative lasers, can often trigger herpes outbreaks. To avoid severe scaring and complications of a *herpes infection*, oral antiviral medication is given to all patients with a history of herpes outbreaks in the intended treatment area.

Patients who smoke or have taken oral retinoids, like *Accutane*, within the past year should not undergo ablative procedures due to poor healing and an increased risk of scarring.

A requirement of hair removal lasers is the presence of dark hairs. Therefore patients are instructed to avoid shaving, waxing, plucking, electrolysis, and/or bleaching of the hairs before treatment. Avoiding sun exposure is also recommended for at least two weeks preceding treatment because hair removal lasers cannot distinguish between the pigment in tanned skin and dark hair. For this reason, it is sometimes advisable to pretreat darkly pigmented skin with bleaching agents to lessen the possibility of postprocedure hypopigmentation (loss of color).

Anesthesia

Discomfort is usually *minor*, both during the procedure and throughout the recovery phase. In most cases, laser procedures are performed using a topical anesthetic cream. For laser hair removal, specialized cooling methods are used to gently chill the skin to minimize discomfort. For more extensive and lengthy ablative laser procedures, the physician may opt for local anesthesia with monitored intravenous sedation or general anesthesia.

PROCEDURE/TECHNIQUES

Laser procedures are done on an outpatient basis, in a physician's office, or in an accredited and licensed ambulatory surgical center. Patients may go home the same day.

The choice of the laser depends on many factors, including the target tissue, the expectations of the patient, and the surgeon's experience.

After the patient is prepped, a hand-held wand, which is connected to the laser machine, is used to emit a precise beam across the target tissue.

The time required for a laser treatment varies according to the patient's needs, the physician's/operator's ability, the procedure being performed, and the size of the treatment area. Hair removal done on the upper lip can take five minutes, whereas a full-face ablative resurfacing procedure may take up to two hours.

DRESSINGS AND WOUND CARE

Depending on the type of laser used, the depth of penetration, and the individual's ability to heal, a pink surface color may remain for several days to several months. For those patients who experience discomfort or **edema**, an ice pack wrapped in a soft cloth may be applied to the treated area.

Ablative Laser Procedures

Due to the depth of the exfoliation of the ablative procedure, the treated skin will weep until the surface regenerates a new epidermis (usually for about one week) and should be treated with care. Therefore, to keep the wound moist, a dressing, consisting of ointment and/or nonadherent gauze, is applied (Figure 8–12).

If the face has been bandaged, the first dressing change is done in the physician's office within the first 24 hours, then every 1 to 2 days for approximately 7 days or until the skin surface is completely reepithelialized. The wound should be cleaned with cotton balls soaked with the prescribed cleansing solution and blotted dry before applying the ointment, if so prescribed.

Nonablative Laser Procedures

Although there may be some mild redness for a few hours, nonablative laser treatments do not damage the epidermis, do not exfoliate, and therefore no dressings are required.

Sutures

None.

Bathing and Hair Care

With ablative laser resurfacing, the patient may be able to wash and care for the treated skin after the first week. With nonablative laser treatments, bathing and hair care can typically resume the day of laser treatment.

Figure 8–12

Raw surface several days after CO_2 ablative laser treatment. Reprinted with the permission of the American Academy of Dermatology. All rights reserved.

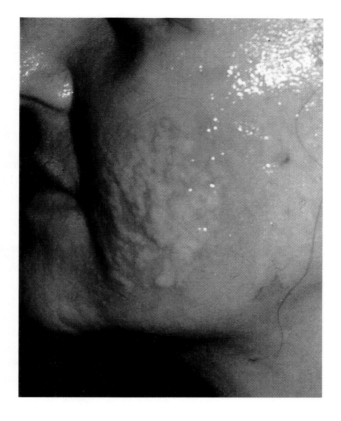

Soaking in bathtubs, steam baths, and sauna baths should be delayed until the skin is reepithelialized—usually about one week; no hair coloring or stripping should be performed until cleared by the treating physician. Assuming the treated skin has been reepithelialized, this is usually allowed after the third week postoperative.

Makeup

Ablative Laser Procedures

Assuming that the treated skin has reepithelialized, makeup can be worn about 7 to 14 days after an ablative laser treatment. Patients should not apply cosmetics until the crust/scabs on the wound have disappeared. Most women are able to apply *camouflage makeup* after two weeks so the pinkness is less noticeable. In rare cases, the skin may be too sensitive to wear certain makeup. In such cases, hypoallergenic makeup may be prescribed.

Nonablative Laser Procedures

Mild redness may persist for a few hours with nonablative techniques and makeup may usually be applied immediately after the laser treatment.

Sun Protection

It is important to avoid unprotected, direct sun exposure for several months after laser treatment. If patients must be outdoors for prolonged periods of time, it is recommended that they wear hats and sunscreen lotions with an SPF of 15 or greater. If laser skin resurfacing was performed in the areas around the eyes, high-quality sunglasses with UV filters should be worn.

POSTPROCEDURE SKIN/TISSUE CHANGES

Posttreatment skin changes, including erythema and pigmentary changes, depend on the type of laser, duration of treatment, the area treated, intensity of the beam, skin pigmentation, and whether an ablative or nonablative laser is used. These skin changes may remain for several days to months posttreatment.

The presence of pain, redness, swelling, and/or pus may occur with infection. If present, particularly after the first week posttreatment, the physician should be notified.

Ablative Laser Procedures

Due to the superficial burn on the surface of the skin, patients may experience some discomfort and pain immediately after the laser resurfacing treatment, which may last about 7 to 10 days posttreatment. During the first 2 weeks after ablation laser treatment, a significant amount of redness and weeping of the skin can be expected. This is associated with some skin edema, oozing, and *eschars* (scabs) on the treated skin. Crusting will normally disappear within 10 days. It is important not to pick these eschars off, as doing so may increase the likelihood for posttreatment scarring.

As new skin cells develop during the healing process, a smooth, fresh layer of skin slowly emerges. Initially the skin is smooth and looks good due to swelling. After 3 months, most of the swelling has disappeared and wrinkles may appear to be returning, but collagen remodeling leads to subtle and more permanent improvement. The full impact of the laser may not be apparent for 6 to 12 months.

Erythema is usual and should not be regarded as a complication of ablative laser treatment; it typically lasts two to three months and can be camouflaged with cosmetics. Milia and acne may occur, especially if occlusive ointments are used after laser treatment.

Some patients may experience transient *hyperpigmentation* (an increase in color). These pigmentary changes usually resolve in several months; however, bleaching creams may enhance improvement. *Hypopigmentation* (lightening of skin) is less common early in the healing but can develop after a year and may be permanent.

Nonablative Laser Procedures

By virtue of its mechanism of action, nonablative lasers do not exfoliate, and thus there is no weeping of the treated skin. *Erythema* is also unusual.

One unwanted side effect from nonablative lasers is posttreatment hyperpigmentation. Hence, if a patient is known to get dark marks on his or her skin as a result of injury or acne, a two-week regimen of bleaching agents and/or retinoids, like Retin-A, may be used to lessen this possibility. Some patients of color may experience transient hyperpigmentation, but these pigmentary changes usually resolve spontaneously or with the help of a bleaching cream. These changes are rarely permanent. Hypopigmentation (lightening of skin) is less common but will improve with time.

Laser Hair Removal

After *laser hair removal,* the patient's skin will usually be **erythematous** and edematous, but this will disappear in short order. On occasion, small crusting or milia may appear around the hair follicles. Though complications with laser hair removal are rare, there is a minimal chance of scarring. Pigmentary changes may occur at the site(s) being treated. In most cases, changes in pigmentation will resolve during the natural healing process.

Scars

The risk of scarring may be increased in patients who develop secondary bacterial infection after laser treatment. With proper precautions, including the avoidance of pretreatment use of oral retinoids, this is extremely rare. Good wound care after laser surgery can also help minimize the risk of scarring.

POSTPROCEDURE ACTIVITIES

If the procedure was done on the head, neck, or face, it is recommended that patients keep their head elevated for several days by sitting in a recliner or using multiple pillows. Patients should also avoid swimming and contact sports before the treated skin is completely reepithelialized.

Although patients can return to work as soon as they feel comfortable, they should allow 7 to 10 days before returning to normal physical activity.

Ablative Laser Procedures

If there are no signs or symptoms of infection, facial massage can resume about 10 to 14 days posttreatment. Body massage can resume so long as extra care is exercised to avoid any pressure on the face while in the **prone position**. Scalp massage can be done after ablative laser treatment if care is taken not to manipulate the treated area on the face.

Nonablative Laser Procedures

Because the epidermis remains dry, facial and body massage can resume immediately after nonablative laser skin resurfacing.

Eye Protection

Invisible laser beams do not produce a bright light that would cause the blinking reflex and, therefore, chances of injury are great. *Visible laser beams* can be so intense that it can do damage faster than a blink of an eye. Proper protective eyewear is thus essential during the procedure for both the patient and the staff.

SOME RISKS AND POSSIBLE COMPLICATIONS

Although generally safe, as with any surgical procedure, laser treatment in *aesthetic medicine* has some potential risks and complications; however, complications tend to be minimal and infrequent when performed by or under the supervision of an experienced physician. They are further minimized with meticulous pretreatment and posttreatment wound care. Although rare, the following may occur:

- Infection
- Changes with skin pigmentation
- Scarring
- Reactivation of herpes simplex infections

Chapter 9

Sclerotherapy

■ Harry Sendzischew, MD

Sclerotherapy is the obliteration of certain veins by injecting a **sclerosing solution** directly into the lumen of the vein, causing the vein to disappear within a matter of weeks. For the past 70 years it has been the gold standard for the treatment of spider veins and some varicose veins. Today, it is also used in the treatment of facial veins, which differ from spider veins and varicose veins.

Spider veins, also known as *telangiectasias,* are small, dilated, superficial blood vessels that appear red or blue. They may be short, unconnected lines each about the size of a hair, or connected in a "sunburst" pattern. Sometimes they may branch off from a varicose vein. They may also look like a spider web or a tree with branches.

They can appear in a small area and are not very noticeable, or they can cover a large area of skin and be quite noticeable. Although spider veins typically appear on the legs, they can also appear on the face or elsewhere. Although smaller blue veins may sometimes cause pain, the larger vessels are more likely to cause discomfort. Spider veins on the nose or cheeks of fair-skinned people may be related to sun exposure.

The exact cause of spider veins is not completely understood; however, a number of factors contribute to their development, including heredity (identical twins can be affected in the same area of the body), weight gain, certain medications, and occupations that require prolonged sitting or standing.

They appear more often in women. In some women, spider veins may become noticeable in their teenage years. However, most tend to appear in women in their mid-thirties and early forties. **Hormones** may also play a role in their development (i.e., puberty, birth control pills, hormone replacement therapy, or pregnancy). In most cases, those that surface during pregnancy will decrease on their own, but they will not fully disappear. They may also appear after an injury or as a result of wearing tight girdles or hosiery with tight rubber bands.

Varicose veins are usually dilated more than a fourth-inch in diameter. They are darker in color and tend to bulge above the skin surface; they may occur along with spider veins. Varicose veins typically cause more discomfort than spider veins. They are usually related to more serious venous disorders. Varicose veins occur from the backward flow of blood in the legs caused by damaged or diseased valves in the vein. In the majority of cases, these leg markings can be unsightly and may be associated with *symptoms* such as swelling, cramping, aching, throbbing, and fatigue of the legs and feet. Treatment, as with spider veins, is often sought for cosmetic reasons.

Facial veins, also known as **reticular veins**, are small, prominent veins that usually occur around the eyes but they may also appear at the nasolabial folds. They are thicker than spider veins and thinner than varicose veins.

INDICATIONS

Spider Veins *(Telangiectasias)*

Unsightliness is the most common reason for seeking treatment; however, spider veins may also be removed to alleviate symptoms that range from a dull throbbing pain to a burning sensation or cramps. Treatment does not prevent the development of new spider veins; however, the removal of existing veins can dramatically improve the appearance of the affected area as well as possibly slow the development of new spider veins (Figure 9–1).

Varicose Veins

For some patients, sclerotherapy can be used to treat varicose veins. However, *surgical treatment* is often necessary (i.e., surgically **ligation** of veins [tying of] or **vein stripping** [pulling out] through small incisions [Figure 9–2]). Common side effects of the two include scars, sensory deficit, and prolonged recovery time. These procedures may require a hospital visit as well as sedation or general anesthesia.

Facial Veins (Reticular Veins)

Although there is usually no pain or visual problems associated with facial veins, they project shades of blue or green that can be esthetically displeasing. Other treatment options include lasers (Figure 9–3).

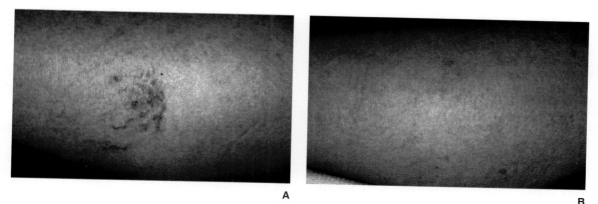

Figure 9–1

A, Spider veins. B, Spider veins after sclerotherapy. Reprinted with the permission of the American Academy of Dermatology. All rights reserved.

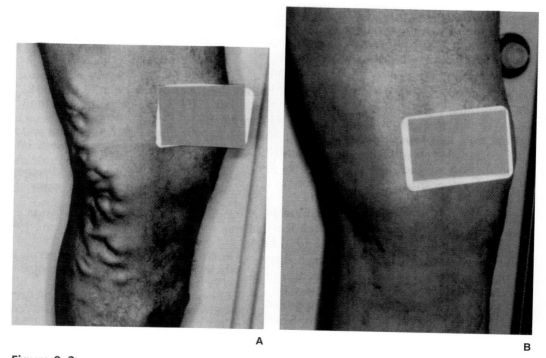

Figure 9–2

A, Varicose vein of the leg. B, Same leg after *vein stripping.* Reprinted with permission from *The American Journal of Cosmetic Surgery.*

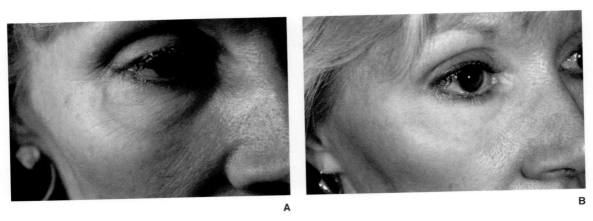

A   **B**

Figure 9–3

A, Facial veins. B, Facial veins after sclerotherapy. Reprinted with the permission of the American Academy of Dermatology. All rights reserved.

MECHANISM OF ACTION AND TARGET TISSUES

Using a microthin needle, a sclerosing solution is injected directly into the lumen of the vein. The solution thickens the blood and irritates the **intima** (lining) of the vein, causing it to swell and stick together. The vein blanches and, over a period of weeks, the vessel turns into scar tissue that is eventually absorbed, becoming barely noticeable or invisible. There are several such solutions, which act slightly different. These solutions are **hypertonic** saline, a detergent-based solution or a fatty acid solution. All of these solutions are mild enough to be relatively painless, yet predictable in their sclerosing effect. The choice depends on several factors, including the size of the vessel to be injected.

Aside from facial veins, spider veins and varicose veins may recur. It may seem that a previously injected vessel has recurred, when, in fact, a new vein has appeared in the same area. Recurrence may be new vessels or may be due to an underlying problem with the venous system. Occasionally larger varicose veins are underneath or associated with spider veins. In such cases, some physicians believe that these larger vessels should be treated before the spider veins are treated. This will lessen the chance of recurrence in the same area.

PREPROCEDURE CONSIDERATIONS

Patients with circulatory problems, heart conditions, **thrombophlebitis, pulmonary emboli**, a tendency to form blood clots easily, or diabetes may be advised against treatment. **Coumadin** therapy, a **blood thinner**, is a relative contraindication to sclerotherapy. The deep venous system must be unobstructed. There must be an absence of **cellulitis** and there must be an absence of inflammation in the superficial or deep veins.

Anesthesia

Anesthesia is not necessary; the procedure is performed in the surgeon's office or an outpatient surgical facility. The solution is usually diluted with lidocaine.

PROCEDURE/TECHNIQUES

Spider Veins

Each injection covers about 1 inch of the vein. In any one-treatment session a number of vessels can be injected; there can be anywhere from 5 to 40 injections per session. A typical sclerotherapy session is relatively quick, lasting from 15 to 45 minutes (Figure 9–4).

Only about 50 to 70 percent of the treated vessels will be permanently gone after the first treatment. Three to four treatments are generally required for optimal results. In general, if a second series of injections is required, a one-month healing interval should pass before reinjecting the same area.

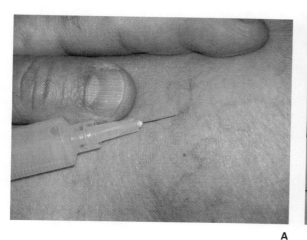
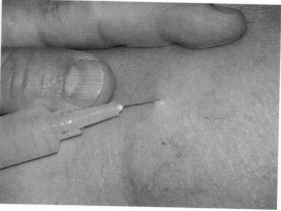

A   B

Figure 9–4

A, A spider vein being injected with a 35-gauge needle. B, Same patient immediately after injection. Reprinted with permission of Harry Sendzischew, MD. All rights reserved.

Facial Veins (Reticular Veins)

Although sclerotherapy has been used successfully for more than 75 years to remove unwanted spider veins and varicose veins on the legs, it has only recently been found to be safe to remove unwanted facial veins, which are different from spider veins.

In one study of approximately 50 patients whose facial veins were treated with injections, sclerotherapy was found to be effective in permanently removing facial veins after only one treatment session. Hyperpigmentation, or darkening of the skin at the treatment site, is very rare. The complete disappearance of the facial veins was observed within two months after treatment for all patients; no new veins appeared in the skin around the eyes where the facial veins were removed.

DRESSINGS AND WOUND CARE

Injected sites on the legs are covered with compression tape (Figure 9–5). For multiple areas in legs, compression with an ace bandage or support hose stocking may be required (Figure 9–6). An ice pack is applied to the treated area for the first 12 hours, and patients are instructed to stay off of their feet until the following morning. If ace bandages are applied, they are removed on the following morning.

After the first day postinjection, warm compresses may be applied to the treated area 2 to 3 times per day, for 15 minutes, for a period of

Figure 9–5

Compression tape over injection site. Reprinted with the permission of Harry Sendzischew, MD. All rights reserved.

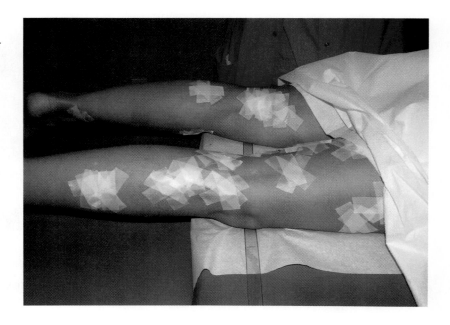

Figure 9–6

Ace bandage compression for multiple areas on legs. Reprinted with the permission of Harry Sendzischew, MD. All rights reserved.

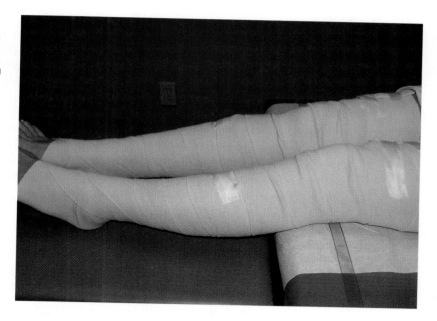

7 to 10 days. For facial veins, a small compression dressing may be applied over the treated area for the first 12 hours after injections.

Sutures

No sutures are used.

Bathing and Hair Care

Bathing is usually permitted after the dressing is removed. Washing the hair can usually be done the day after the injections.

Makeup

For treated legs, camouflage makeup can be applied to cover bruising. Facial makeup can usually be applied gently after the dressing has been removed.

POSTPROCEDURE SKIN/TISSUE CHANGES

Treated veins will look worse before they begin to look better. When the compression dressings are removed, bruising and reddish areas at the injection sites may be present. The bruises will diminish within

10 to 30 days. In many cases, there may be some residual brownish pigmentation (when blood escapes from treated veins), which may take 6 to 12 months to completely fade. This is probably from iron in the blood. Red, raised, hive-like areas may occasionally appear at the sites of injection, which typically disappear within days.

Small, painful ulcers can appear at the treatment sites (rare), either immediately or within a few days of injection. These occur when some of the solution escapes into the surrounding skin or enters a tiny artery at the treatment site. They can be successfully treated.

Muscle cramps almost always occur when the injection solution is hypertonic saline and usually go away quickly. Swelling of the ankles or feet may occur with treatment of veins in the lower leg and/or as a result of the compression dressing.

Scars

In the hands of experienced physicians, external scarring is rare.

POSTPROCEDURE ACTIVITIES

Patients are advised to refrain from vigorous activities for the first 24 hours; they should avoid activities that put pressure on the treated area, heavy lifting, prolonged sitting, standing or squatting, and pounding-type exercises such as jogging. As with all procedures involving the skin, patients should avoid unprotected exposure to direct sunlight.

With proper dressing and precautions, patients can resume work and all normal activities within a few days posttreatment.

SOME RISKS AND POSSIBLE COMPLICATIONS

Complications from sclerotherapy are extremely rare when performed by a qualified physician; however, they may occur. Possible risks include the following:

- Irregular brownish pigmentation around the treated skin
- Allergic reactions to sclerosing agents
- Inflammation of treated blood vessels
- Lumps in injected vessels, particularly the larger veins
- Small, painful ulcers at the treatment sites
- Telangiectatic matting—fine reddish blood vessels may occasionally appear around the treated area, requiring further treatment (Figure 9–7)

Figure 9–7

Matting after sclerotherapy—
note the discoloration from
the previous injections.
Reprinted with the permission
of the American Academy of
Dermatology. All rights reserved.

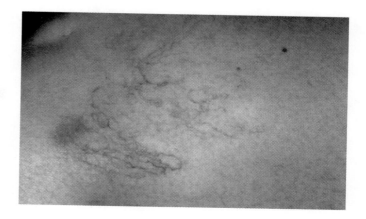

Chapter 10

Permanent Cosmetics

■ Marjorie M. Grimm, CPCP

In 2003 the **Society of Permanent Cosmetic Professionals** (SPCP) conducted *Industry Profile: Vision 2003*, a study accumulating data globally from those who provide permanent cosmetic services. The results of this study revealed that in addition to offering permanent cosmetics, nearly 29 percent are also working as estheticians, 23 percent as cosmetologists, 14 percent are nail technicians, 13 percent electrologist, 11 percent nurses, 10 percent are traditional tattoo artists, and less than 1 percent represent those who are physicians. It is regulated in most areas throughout the United States and abroad.

Permanent cosmetics is the technique of injecting (tattooing) pigment directly into the skin and is also referred to as "**permanent makeup**," "**micropigmentation**," or "**dermagraphics**." This service has appealed to many professionals from the tattooing and beauty industries, and it is rapidly gaining popularity as an alternative to conventional makeup as well as an adjunct in *aesthetic medicine* and **reconstructive surgery**.

INDICATIONS

Reconstructive Indications

Nipple-Areolar Reconstruction

To alleviate the physical and psychological distortion, **nipple-areola** reconstruction is indicated in patients with loss from mastectomy, trauma, or congenital absence. The goal is to recreate a nipple and areola complex that is symmetric with the opposite breast.

Numerous nipple-areola reconstructive techniques exist, including reconstruction with **skin grafts**, local tissue flaps, intradermal tattooing, **cartilage grafts**, tissue-engineered structures, and **nipple-sharing techniques**.

A stable breast mound reconstruction is obtained before nipple-areola reconstruction. A period of two to three months is usually allowed for settling of the reconstructed breast mound before the nipple-areolar complex is reconstructed and/or tattooed.

For optimal results in aesthetics of the reconstructed breast, both the nipple and areola should be reconstructed.

Nipple Reconstruction
The most challenging aspect of nipple reconstruction is the creation of a projecting nipple, with texture, dimensions, and contour similar to the opposite nipple. The nipple is usually reconstructed with local tissue flaps that are configured to give projection and mimic the nipple. Even so, loss of nipple projection is not uncommon several years after surgery. However, there is less of this occurrence with the use of certain flaps.

Recipients of permanent tattooing for cosmetic reasons are referred to as **clients;** when done for reconstructive reasons, they are referred to as *patients.*

Although pigmented skin grafts from the contra-lateral nipple-areola complex or the medial thigh-vulva area are often used, advances in tattooing have now become a popular option to reconstruct the nipple-areolar complex. When performed by a properly trained and experienced technician, it is relatively simple, easy to perform, readily correctable, and requires no significant patient participation or convalescence. Tattooing affords greater precision of control over size, definition of the contour, and color match to the opposite side.

Scar Camouflage

Endless colors are now available to camouflage scars to blend in with the surrounding tissue.

Cosmetic Indications

Active people involved with sports, outdoor hobbies, and/or rushed schedules, those with arthritis, allergies to conventional makeup products, skin sensitivities, faulty eyesight, poor hand-eye coordination, limited dexterity, and those with other medical conditions may find permanent cosmetics appealing.

Permanent cosmetics can be very subtle or applied more dramatically depending on the client/patient's desires. It is used to enhance certain facial features or to give scar and hypopigmented skin tissue a more natural appearance. Some uses include:

- Eyebrows (Figure 10–1)
- Eyeliner (Figure 10–2)
- Lips (Figure 10–3)
- Skin camouflage (Figure 10–4)
- Areola repigmentation (Figure 10–5)

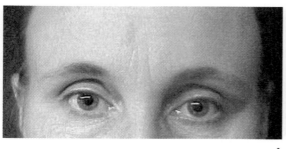 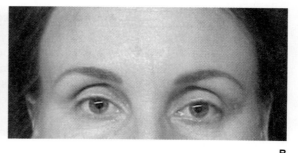

A　　　　　　　　　　　　　　　　　　　　B

Figure 10–1

A, Poorly defined eyebrows. B, Same client after tattooing. Reprinted with permission from Marjorie Grimm at Faces By Design.

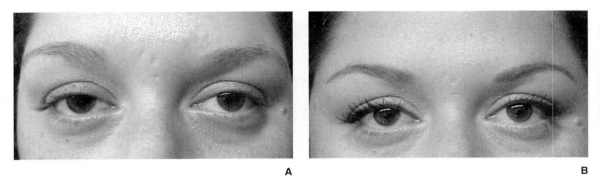

Figure 10–2

A, Eyeliner. B, Same client after tattooing. Reprinted with permission from Marjorie Grimm at Faces By Design.

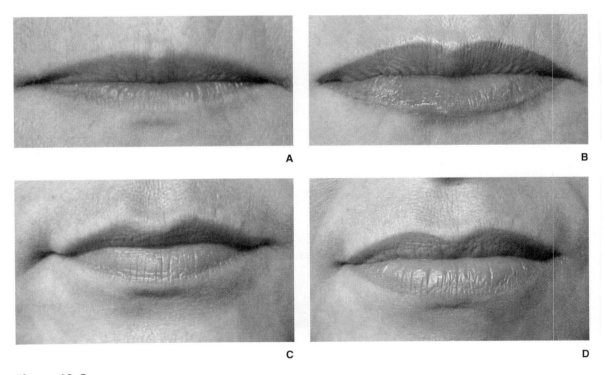

Figure 10–3

A, Lip shaper. B, Same client after tattooing. C, Full lip. D, Same client after tattooing. Reprinted with permission from Marjorie Grimm at Faces By Design.

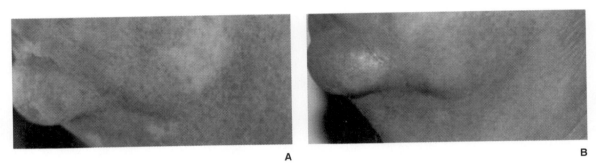

Figure 10–4

A, Hypopigmented skin. B, Same client after tattooing. Reprinted with permission from Mary Jane Haake at Dermigraphics, LLC.

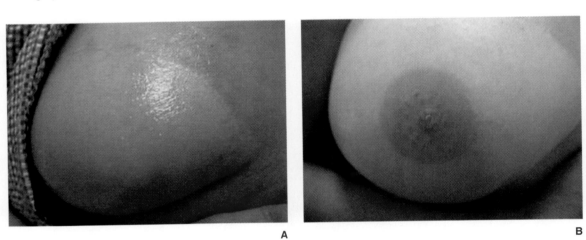

Figure 10–5

A, Breast reconstruction minus the nipple/areolar complex. B, Same patient after tattooing. Reprinted with permission from Liza Sims in Anchorage, Alaska.

MECHANISM OF ACTION AND TARGET TISSUES

Permanent cosmetics are considered permanent because, as with body art tattooing, the pigment is injected directly into the reticular dermis via fine needles that are attached to a coil machine (the machine commonly used for body art tattoos), a rotary machine, or a hand tool (manual method).

Pigment particles used for permanent cosmetics are insoluble in water. Dyes are organic compounds exclusively derived from carbon-based compounds, whereas pigments are finely ground, inorganic oxide-based compounds. Colors made available for purchase by technicians may contain organic or inorganic ingredients, or a combination of both.

PREPROCEDURE CONSIDERATIONS

In most instances, physicians do not perform permanent cosmetic tattooing; they either have a permanent cosmetic technician on staff or refer their patient to an independent professional who is properly trained. Ultimately, if proper sterilization and infection control guidelines are met by the professional, permanent cosmetics are considered relatively safe procedures.

Because of the occasional reaction to a given pigment, some tattooists and physicians may conduct a spot test with the proposed pigments. Although this practice does not preclude the possibility of a reaction at some point in time, and is therefore considered an unreliable indicator, at least one state requires this test by law. Insurance companies and color manufacturers vary on the requirement. Nonmedical technicians may or may not be agreeable to "reading" a spot test, as this diagnosis of skin condition in many professional circles is considered to be more appropriately accomplished by a qualified physician.

The shape and placement of the pigment is equally as important as selecting the right color. A well-trained professional will have a thorough working knowledge of facial morphology and color theory as it relates to placing tattoo color into an existing skin color. Tattoo color plus skin tone produces a final version of the color that will be different from that seen in a container.

Finally, given the sometimes-unregulated nature of the industry, it is crucial to select a properly trained and experienced professional. Clients/patients should ask for the tattooist's portfolio to examine preprocedure and postprocedure photos of their work. They should also request evidence of a business license, fundamental or advanced training (if the procedure is advanced in nature such as camouflage scar and skin work or areola repigmentation), and of **Occupational Safety and Health Administration** (OSHA) blood-borne pathogens standard training.

Those with medical conditions that could preclude proper healing are directed to consult with their physicians before proceeding.

Anesthesia

Most patients/clients will experience some discomfort, which will vary with their pain threshold, the effectiveness of anesthetics used, and the skills of the technician. Typically, a topical anesthetic cream is applied before and during these procedures that provides sufficient anesthesia. However, if warranted, and if the procedure is being conducted in a medical facility, a physician may administer a local anesthetic or a nerve block.

PROCEDURE/TECHNIQUES

The process includes an initial consultation, the application of pigment, and at least one or more follow-up visits to ensure the design and color has healed to the client's satisfaction.

The procedure involves the use of a hand-held machine or manual device (Figure 10–6), with an 8- or 12-gauge sterilized needle(s) whose action facilitates the pigment into the dermal layer of the skin. As the needle penetrates the skin, a small amount of bleeding may occur.

This procedure generally takes one to two and one-half hours to complete. The actual tattooing time is normally minimal compared with the preparation time spent during the consultation process (forms, photos, and color selection,) and preprocedure design work. At the end of the procedure, the skin is washed and an ointment is applied.

Figure 10–6

Tattooing machine and manual devices. Reprinted with permission from Marjorie Grimm at Faces By Design.

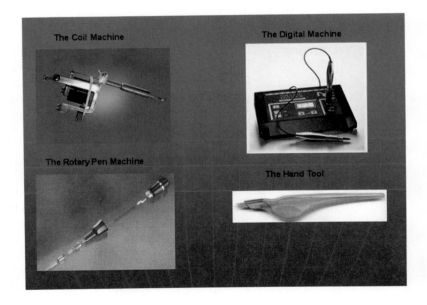

DRESSINGS AND WOUND CARE

It is recommended that clients/patients return home after the procedure and apply *cold compresses* as needed to relieve swelling. During the first 7 to 10 days posttattooing, the procedural area should be kept clean and protected with a thin layer of ointment as it heals.

Sutures

Not applicable.

Bathing and Hair Care

This can resume immediately after the tattooing session. It is recommended that the face is turned away from direct shower spray and that hair shampoo/conditioning products be allowed to drain so that product contact is avoided on the procedure area. The treated area should not be scrubbed or washed with a cloth. Steam baths/saunas, exposure to extreme sunlight, and salt water should be avoided until the treated area(s) are well healed.

Makeup *(Conventional)*

Makeup on or closely adjacent to the tattooed area should be postponed until that area is healed. Because *mascara* tubes contain bacteria, if an eyeliner tattoo procedure has been performed and the client normally wears mascara, a new tube should be purchased and the old one discarded. New lipstick or lip balms should be used over a tattooed lip procedure.

Sun Protection

It is important to avoid unprotected, direct sun exposure for several months after a *permanent cosmetics* procedure. If patients/clients must be outdoors for prolonged periods of time, it is recommended that they wear hats and sunscreen lotions with an SPF of 15 or greater; if the eyebrow or eyelids were done, high-quality sunglasses with UV filters should be worn.

POSTPROCEDURE SKIN/TISSUE CHANGES

Immediately after the procedure, there may be some swelling, slight bruising (typically around the delicate eye area, if any at all), and sensitivity around the treated area. This may last for several hours to several days depending on client factors. Although eyebrows may show little aftereffect other than the prominent color, eyeliner and lips may produce more edema, which may last from 2 to 72 hours.

As the procedural area heals, a scab may form. Although aftercare instructions should preclude scabbing, some clients will produce a slight crust to heavy scab as a natural element of their unique healing process. The eyebrow procedure is more likely to produce a light crust or scab than the eyeliner or lip procedure. If so, it should NOT be peeled off; it should be allowed to exfoliate naturally. During this time, the skin must be kept clean to avoid infection; topical antibiotics or ointments are used to cover the area.

During the healing process, it is important to avoid conventional makeup, direct sunlight, and contact with acid-based facial products, as these elements have an adverse effect on pigment in the treated area.

In the first 6 to 10 days postprocedure, the color may be much darker than expected; this will soften and lighten during the healing process. The implanted color is usually not perfect after the first procedure, and the color may fade and need to be touched up at the follow-up visit. The healing process involves the natural exfoliation of the epidermis. During the procedure, approximately 10 to 20 percent of the pigment remains trapped in this epidermal layer and is expected to shed with the dead skin cells. This results in less concentration of pigment that is retained in the dermal layer of the skin, thus a lighter healed color. Around 4 to 6 weeks after the initial procedure, a follow-up visit is scheduled to make any needed changes to the pigmentation.

Over time with factors such as sun exposure and contact with facial products, pigments begin to fade. A shift in true color can be avoided by initially using a color that is complimentary to the client's skin tone. For instance a warm-based eyebrow pigment (red) applied to a cool (green) skin tone creates color balance and little change in true color is expected, only a lightening effect over time. Adversely, a warm-based eyebrow pigment (red) applied to a warm skin (red or pink) tone creates color imbalance and may result in an orange undertone as the pigment ages. Color selection is critical to a desirable color aging process.

If patients/clients are dissatisfied with the results, it may be difficult, but possible, to remove the pigment with dermabrasion or laser skin resurfacing. Many permanent cosmetic professionals perform "tattoo lightening," enabling adjustments to design and color by overtattooing with a saline or salt paste solution, thereby lifting the pigments to the surface of the skin to be discarded in the healing/scabbing process. Success of tattoo lightening or removal by any method is largely dependent on the color, color composition, and depth of the pigment. Technical advances have been made in the medical tattoo removal arena with lasers; however, it is important to match the right tattoo color with the appropriate laser and the right skin tone to avoid hyperpigmentation/hypopigmentation or scarring of the skin tissue in the process of the removal treatment.

Scars

Although extremely rare, a potential for scarring exists. This is generally not seen in the hands of skilled tattooists, but for those who have a predisposition to hypertrophic scars and/or keloid formation, greater care should be taken or the procedure refused in some instances.

POSTPROCEDURE ACTIVITIES

Normal activities may be resumed immediately. It is always advisable that patients/clients have permanent cosmetic procedures performed at a time when there is no immediate forthcoming important social or business event planned.

People with tattoos should notify their physician if a **magnetic resonance imaging (MRI)** is planned because some tattoos have metallic-base dyes, which can interact with the extremely strong magnetic field created by the MRI.

SOME RISKS AND POSSIBLE COMPLICATIONS

Most risks and complications known to be associated with permanent cosmetics are minor when performed by a properly trained and experienced permanent cosmetic professional. Some include:

- Infections
- Scarring
- Allergic reactions

Section Three

Surgical Aesthetic Procedures

Chapter 11

Face-Lift Rhytidectomy

■ Leslie H. Stevens, MD, FACS

The medical term for face-lift is **rhytidectomy**; it is derived from the Latin word **rhytid** (wrinkle) and *ectomy* (to remove). It is one of the most popular and satisfying cosmetic surgical procedures.

Although the incisions for a face-lift extend up into the hairline, it does virtually nothing to the upper part of the face. Thus, a face-lift is often combined with a forehead-lift, eyelid surgery, and/or facial liposuction. Concurrent with a face-lift, "skin resurfacing" can be used to "fine-tune" the facial skin (e.g., a chemical peel, dermabrasion, or laser resurfacing). *Rhytidectomy* and skin resurfacing compliment each other but one is not a substitute for the other. Resurfacing best treats superficial lines and wrinkles, pigmentation, and irregularities.

INDICATIONS

Rhytidectomy is most effective in eliminating loose skin and deep wrinkles in the lower third of the face and neck areas; it can give definition to the jaw line (jowls) and remedy **nasolabial folds** that run from the corner of the nose to the corner of the mouth. It can also eliminate those vertical "cords" in the neck that are caused by prominent medial borders of the platysma muscle. Fatty neck tissue can also be remedied during a face-lift with liposuction or sharp resection of the **submental** fat pad.

Most face-lifts are done on patients in their 40s to 60s, but it is not unusual for a healthy 80-year-old to have a face-lift.

MECHANISM OF ACTION AND TARGET TISSUES

Rhytidectomy smoothes loose facial and neck skin by any combination of the following: removing excess fat, removing excess skin, and tightening underlying muscles. There are basically three face-lift techniques and a combination thereof, which are based on the depth of the dissection plane. The dissection planes are superficial, medium, and deep. The remaining skin flap is then redraped over the underlying support structure and secured with complex suturing.

PREPROCEDURE CONSIDERATIONS

Because the *rhytidectomy* incision may extend into the scalp, patients with very short hair may be advised to grow their hair to cover the resulting incision in the scalp while it heals. Optimal healing is enhanced with proper preoperative and postoperative skin care. *Smoking cessation is mandatory* for at least one to two weeks before surgery because smoking inhibits blood flow to the skin and may delay the healing process or even cause loss of skin.

Regardless of the type of anesthesia used, or where the surgery is performed, patients should arrange for someone to drive them home after surgery as well as someone to stay with them to help them with their daily activities for one to two days. It is not unusual for patients to stay up to several nights at a recovery facility after the operation.

Anesthesia

Although many face-lifts are performed under local anesthesia with intravenous sedation, some surgeons prefer **general anesthesia**. The final choice will depend on the patient's wish, the extent of the surgery, ancillary procedures, and/or the surgeon's preference. Those patients done under local anesthesia with IV sedation will be awake but relaxed. Although they may not feel any pain, the patient may feel some tugging and occasional discomfort. Those patients done under general anesthesia will sleep throughout the procedure.

PROCEDURE/TECHNIQUES

Rhytidectomy is a major operative procedure that can be performed in an outpatient surgical center or an office-based facility; others prefer the hospital, where their patients have a brief stay.

There are several *rhytidectomy* techniques, which depend on the depth of the dissection plane: 1) the "classic" plane that only involves a skin flap (superficial plane); 2) the **SMAS**, or **superficial musculoaponeurotic system** (mid-plane); 3) the subperiosteal face-lift (deep plane); and 4) a combination of these techniques. A popular combined technique is called a composite or deep plane *rhytidectomy* where the skin and SMAS are lifted together as one unit.

The superficial (classic) face-lift, which involves the subcutaneous dissection and skin flap advancement, is effective for the ideal face-lift candidate with excellent bone structure, minimal fat deposits, and no platysma bands. The SMAS technique can be applied for deeper soft tissue defects such as platysma bands and excess *submental* and submandibular fat deposits. The **subperiosteal** technique can restore the cheek contour by lifting the cheek pad, thereby softening the nasolabial fold (the fold running from the corner of the nose to the corner of the mouth).

Regardless of the technique, for the most part, they all share the common principle of camouflaging the incisions by placing them in natural creases of the skin and within the scalp. The incision begins within the **temporal scalp**, several centimeters superior to the ear. It then continues in the caudal direction, along the natural contour of the anterior margin of the ear, going under the ear lobe and extending behind the ear to finish at or within the hairline behind the ear. Some surgeons place a portion of the incision behind the **tragus**, (the cartilaginous flap at the front of the ear between the rim and ear lobe). This helps to minimize the amount of visible scar. In some instances a small incision is made beneath the chin for removing fatty tissue in that area and/or for repairing the "turkey neck" irregularity caused by band-like structures of the underlying platysma muscle.

Through the incisions, the skin flap is dissected from the underlying tissues (Figure 11–1). If needed, the muscles and sagging tissue are then tightened, excess fat is cut or suctioned, and the excess skin is trimmed and redraped (Figure 11–2).

Before closure, a small, thin drainage tube may be temporarily placed under the skin, behind the ear to drain any blood or fluid that might collect under the skin flap. The remaining tissue is then closed with complex stitching—fine, nonabsorbable sutures on the skin and thick nonabsorbable sutures or metal clips to close the scalp wound (Figure 11–3).

Depending on the depth of dissection and/or complexity of the procedure, face-lift surgery generally requires approximately two hours to perform. After adequate recovery room observation, the patient is usually permitted to go home, although some patients may stay overnight in the hospital or recovery facility.

At the end of the face-lift procedure, the scalp and face are washed gently with saline or an antiseptic solution. Then, using a large-toothed comb, snarls, tangles, and dried blood are gently removed from the scalp.

In men, the incision is sometimes modified just anterior to the ear to preserve the hair-bearing definition of their sideburns.

Figure 11–1

Dissection of the *superficial plane* (skin only).

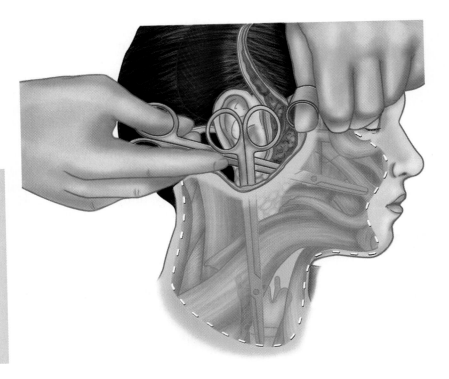

Rhytidectomy Techniques
- The superficial plane ("classic") technique that only involves a skin flap
- The mid-plane technique (SMAS technique)
- The subperiosteal technique
- Deep-plane or composite technique
- A combination of these techniques
- The "thread lift"

Figure 11–2

The loose skin is pulled, re-draped, and trimmed before suturing.

Figure 11–3

Sutured wound with drain (if used) in place.

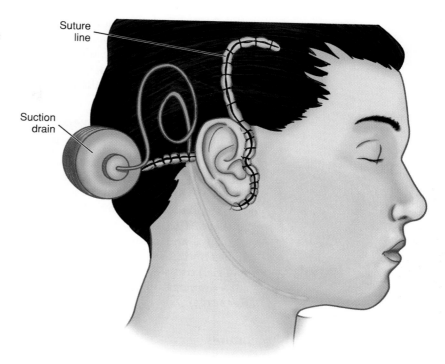

Suture line

Suction drain

Thread Lift

The "thread" face-lift procedure, also known as a ***thread lift,*** is a simple, minimally invasive, FDA-approved procedure using the *innovative* placement of subcutaneous sutures. The sutures are made of clear polypropylene material with tiny, evenly spaced barbs or cogs. These "threads" are placed in the subcutaneous layer (through small incisions), and arranged in an umbrella-like fashion with sufficient tension to gently suspend/lift the sagging tissues. The placement and number of sutures will vary from patient to patient.

These "threads" are best used for subtle repositioning of saggy cheeks, jowls, or eyebrows in individuals with good elasticity of the skin. The body surrounds each "thread" with collagen. The *thread lift* does not replace a traditional face-lift because it cannot fully correct too much sagging. Thus it is not as effective for a neck-lift.

This procedure is performed under local anesthesia. If done by a properly trained and experienced physician this procedure is quick, effective, and safe. Surgery time is usually under one hour, but it will vary on the area treated and the number of threads used. In most cases, there is minimal discomfort with some slight bruising and swelling. Ice compresses are recommended for the first 48 hours. Patients can usually return to work or normal activities in a few days.

The length of time the results last depends on the age of the patient, the degree of sagging, and the number of threads used. Additional threads may be added with time, as needed.

DRESSINGS AND WOUND CARE

The suture lines are covered with flat cotton wedges that are soaked in mineral oil or antibiotic ointment. This is then covered with nonabsorbent gauze that is secured with stocking net dressing, which also cushions the skin flaps and helps eliminate dead space beneath the skin flaps. The dressing may be changed or removed within one to three days and changed as needed. A scarf may be worn to cover stitches until they are removed. Some surgeons prefer not to use any (material) dressing.

If a drainage tube was inserted, it will be removed one to two days after surgery.

Sutures

Sutures are removed in stages: most of the nonabsorbable sutures anterior to the ears are removed in 4 to 5 days; the sutures behind the ear can be removed in 9 to 10 days; and the sutures or staples in the scalp can be left in a few days longer.

Bathing and Hair Care

Many physicians prefer to keep the dressing and incisions dry until the sutures are removed. Others allow their patients to resume showering within the first three days postoperative. Steam baths and saunas should be avoided for several months or until cleared by the surgeon.

Shampooing, hair care, and gentle brushing can resume as early as the second postoperative day. Due to temporary numbness around the ears and temples, and the risk of a burn, a hair dryer, if used, should be set at medium-to-cool heat. No hair coloring or stripping should be performed until cleared by the surgeon. Assuming the wounds have been reepithelialized, this is usually allowed after the third week postoperative.

Makeup

After about one week, the patient may be permitted to wear makeup, which will help conceal discoloration and/or **ecchymosis** (bruising).

Patients should be especially gentle with the face and hair because the skin will be tender and numb.

Special camouflage makeup can mask most ecchymosis. Makeup may be applied over the skin of the face up to the edge of the surgical scars approximately one to two weeks postoperative. If the skin is sensitive to makeup, hypoallergenic makeup can be applied, except for the suture lines, as early as the third day postoperative.

If only a face-lift was performed, a light cover-up may be applied to the eyelids as early as three to four days postoperative. Eyelid makeup, including mascara, eye shadow, eyeliner, and artificial eyelashes, may also be applied four days after the procedure. Makeup should be thoroughly removed at the end of the day.

Earrings should be avoided until sensation has *returned* to the earlobes.

Sun Protection

It is important to avoid unprotected, direct sun exposure for several months after facial surgery. If patients must be outdoors for prolonged periods of time, it is recommended that they wear hats and sunscreen lotions with an SPF of 15 or greater. High-quality sunglasses with UV filters should be worn.

POSTPROCEDURE SKIN/TISSUE CHANGES

When patients have their dressing removed, it is not uncommon for some disappointment and/or depression, which may last for one, maybe two weeks.

Generally, the greatest amount of **edema** (swelling) occurs 24 to 48 hours after surgery. For the first couple of days the facial features may be distorted from asymmetrical **edema** and patients may notice a tight sensation in the neck and under the chin. This causes routine facial movements to be slightly stiff. This feeling may last several weeks and is a normal part of recovery. Cold compresses and sleeping with the head elevated may help minimize this.

When the dressing is removed, the incision lines are quite noticeable. A minor crust may appear on the incisions; however, this is a temporary problem and should be left alone. Picking at the crust may result in scarring. Because the healing process is gradual, it will take several weeks for an accurate picture of the final result; additional minor changes, or settling, may occur over several months as the tissue settles. After the edema and ecchymosis have disappeared, the hair around the temples may be thin and the skin may feel dry and rough for several months.

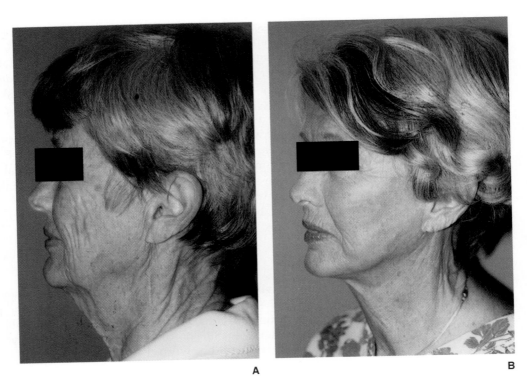

A   B

Figure 11–4

A, Before a face-lift. B, After a face-lift. Photographs courtesy of David Rapaport, MD, plastic surgeon, Park Avenue, New York.

Small superficial sensory nerves are interrupted during a face-lift that results in some degree of numbness along portions of the scalp, cheeks, and neck. This sensory deficit usually returns over several months, but some numbness may last indefinitely.

Because there are many factors involved, it is impossible to state with any degree of accuracy just how long the effects of a face-lift will last. These factors include, but are not limited to, the patient's bone structure, skin type, ability to heal, ethnic background, age and physical condition, lifestyle, preoperative and postoperative sun exposure, and skin elasticity and texture. It has been shown that certain face-lift techniques may last longer or require fewer revisions than others (Figure 11–4).

Scars

In general, scarring is minimal and, because of the strategic placement of the incisions, usually goes unnoticed by the causal observer.

It is very rare for patients to develop *hypertrophic* or *keloid scars* from a face-lift; however, it is recognized that patients of dark skin pigmentation may run a higher risk of developing hypertrophic or keloid scars after this or most any other surgery. If hypertrophy occurs it is most likely to be on the portion of the incision behind the ears.

POSTPROCEDURE ACTIVITIES

Surprisingly, there is little discomfort postoperatively. Walking and mild stretching are encouraged as early as 24 hours after surgery. Patients are instructed to keep their head elevated when lying down or sleeping and to avoid as much activity as possible for the first week after surgery, including driving a car. Strenuous activity and heavy housework should be avoided for at least 3 weeks. Straining, bending, and lifting should be avoided during the first month postoperatively.

Patients should avoid drinking alcohol for the first two weeks postoperative because of the dehydrating and inebriating effect as well as the potential for bleeding due to **vasodilatation** caused by alcohol.

Many patients return to work within two weeks, and by the third week, patients will look and feel much better. In many instances, patients are able to exercise three to four weeks after surgery. Patients are usually able to resume social functions by the third postoperative week.

Unnecessary exposure to direct sunlight is discouraged, and the use of a sun block to protect the skin for several weeks postoperative is encouraged. Aspirin and certain anti-inflammatory medications should be avoided. Any significant pain not readily relieved with pain pills, bleeding, redness, sudden edema, or drainage from the surgical area should be reported to the surgeon immediately.

SOME RISKS AND POSSIBLE COMPLICATIONS

Individuals vary greatly in their anatomy, their physical reactions, and their healing abilities, and the outcome is never completely predictable. Fortunately, when a qualified cosmetic surgeon performs a face-lift, *complications are infrequent* and usually minor. Some potential complications include:

- Hematoma/bleeding
- Alopecia (hair loss) in the temporal area adjacent to the incision line

- Sensory nerve injuries—rare and usually temporary around the ears and cheeks
- Motor nerve injury with temporary or permanent paralysis
- Infection
- Reactions to the anesthesia—rare
- Some skin loss, particularly in smokers

Chapter 12

Forehead-Lift
Brow-Lift

A *forehead-lift* (brow-lift) is a cosmetic or functional surgical procedure that targets the upper third of the face (i.e., forehead and eyebrows). It does absolutely nothing for the middle or lower face. Further, it is important to understand that the texture of the skin will not be altered by a forehead-lift. Thus, it is not uncommon for patients to have concomitant skin resurfacing *(peels/dermabrasion/laser),* face-lift, and/or blepharoplasty to improve the overall texture of the skin as well as to give the face a more youthful appearance.

INDICATIONS

A forehead-lift is used to smooth wrinkles *(rhytids)* and/or to soften deep frown lines and furrows between the eyes and/or to elevate the brow for a more pleasing and restful look.

Eyelid surgery (blepharoplasty) may also be performed at the same time as a forehead-lift, especially if a patient has significant overhang of the upper eyelids. Sometimes, patients who believe they need upper-eyelid surgery find that a forehead-lift better meets their needs (i.e., severely drooping eyebrows can impair the superior field of vision).

Patients who are bald or who have a receding hairline may still be good candidates for a forehead-lift. The surgeon will simply alter the incision location or perform a more conservative operation.

A forehead-lift procedure is usually done between age 40 and 65.

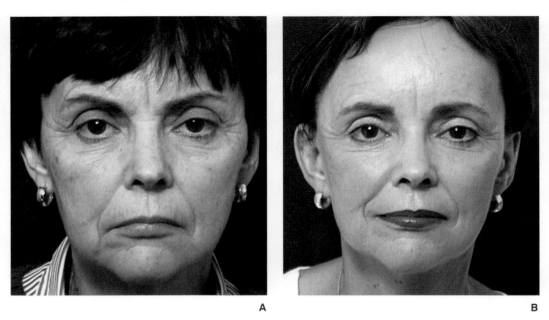

Figure 12–1

A, Laxity of forehead. B, Same patient with a forehead-lift. Photos courtesy of R. Emil Hecht, MD.

MECHANISM OF ACTION AND TARGET TISSUES

There are two main surgical techniques for forehead-lift: the **classic forehead-lift** ("open technique") and the **endoscopic forehead-lift**. The main difference between these two techniques is the placement, number, and size of the incision(s). Both techniques involve the manipulation and excision of muscles and skin that cause the wrinkles, deep frown lines, furrowing, and/or droopy eyebrows. In the *classic technique,* the incision is usually hidden just behind the hairline, extending from ear to ear. In the **endoscopic** method, a viewing instrument (endoscope) allows the procedure to be performed through (multiple) small incisions. Both techniques yield similar results (Figure 12–1).

PREPROCEDURE CONSIDERATIONS

For a better understanding of how a forehead-lift might change a patient's appearance, the cosmetic surgeon places his extended thumbs on the upper and outer edges of the patient's eyebrows and applies gentle, upward pressure. Then, to decide on the placement of the incision(s), the cosmetic surgeon examines the facial structure, the condition of the skin, and the hairline. If the patient's hair is very short, he or she may wish to let it grow out before surgery to hide the resulting scar(s) while it heals.

Anesthesia

Although most forehead-lifts are performed under local anesthesia and intravenous sedation, some surgeons prefer general anesthesia. Patients done under local anesthesia with IV sedation will be awake but relaxed, and although no pain is felt, the patient may feel some tugging or occasional discomfort. The final choice will depend on the patient's wish, the extent of the surgery, ancillary procedures, and/or the surgeon's preference.

PROCEDURE/TECHNIQUES

Both the classic forehead-lift and the endoscopic forehead-lift are usually performed in a surgeon's office-based facility or an outpatient surgery center. However, they are occasionally done in the hospital. Regardless of where the surgery is performed, the patient should make arrangements for transportation to and from surgery and for possible assistance with their daily activities for several days postoperative. Most patients return home the same day.

Both the classic and endoscopic technique requires the same preparation steps as the traditional procedure: the hair is tied back and trimmed behind the hairline where the incisions will be made. Either procedure takes between one to two hours to perform.

The Classic Forehead-Lift

For most patients undergoing the *classic technique*, a coronal incision follows a headphone-like pattern, slightly behind the natural hairline, starting just above ear level and running across the top of the forehead and down to just above the opposite ear (Figure 12–2). If the patient has a high forehead, the mid-portion of the incision is made directly at the hairline to avoid further rising of the forehead. This incision has the advantage of lowering the hairline and generally heals favorably. The disadvantage could be noticeable scarring.

Conversely, if the hairline is very low, the surgeon can raise it by placing the incision near the top of the head. Patients with bald or thinning hair may opt for a mid-scalp incision so the resulting scar

Figure 12–2

Incision placement for the "classic" forehead-lift—from ear to ear.

follows the natural junction of two bones in your skull and is less conspicuous. In some patients with pronounced forehead creases that run across the forehead, the incision can be made within one of these forehead creases. Thus, to the casual observer, the resulting horizontal scar will appear simply as a forehead crease.

The incision is carried down to the **periosteum**. The muscles of the forehead are then altered or released; if needed, the eyebrows are elevated. The excess skin is then trimmed and the surgical margins are closed.

The Endoscopic Lift

Surgical preparation with the endoscopic approach is similar to that of the classic lift. However, as opposed to one long incision, four or five short incisions are made within the scalp, each less than one inch long. A thin viewing endoscopic instrument that is connected to a television monitor is inserted through one of the small incisions. Through one of the other small incisions, another thin instrument is simultaneously inserted, allowing the surgeon to alter or remove underlying tissues. Sometimes, temporary **fixation screws** are placed in the cranium to assist in the repositioning of the muscle tissues. There are a variety of fixation techniques and devices to suspend the forehead tissue.

If a complication should arise during an endoscopic procedure, the surgeon may switch to the classic technique.

DRESSINGS AND WOUND CARE

The dressing will vary among surgeons. A common technique involves the application of a strip of nonadherent gauze over the suture line. This is then covered with ointment; a bulky dressing is applied and secured with a loose-fitting ace bandage.

To minimize swelling, patients should keep their head elevated while lying down or sleeping. Cold compresses may also be applied in some patients to further assist in reducing swelling. Although the surgeon may prescribe pain medication, there is usually little discomfort after a forehead-lift.

Patients are usually seen 1-day postoperative for a wound and dressing check. The bandages are usually removed between 1 to 3 days, sometimes longer. Some surgeons may use drains; if so, they are removed in 24 to 48 hours.

Sutures

In both the classic and endoscopic forehead-lifts, the surgical margins are sutured with nonabsorbable sutures in an *interrupted subcuticular* fashion and/or metal or staples. The stitches or staples are usually removed within the first week postoperative. Sometimes they are removed in stages or left (scalp) up to two weeks after the surgery.

If temporary fixation screws were used, they are removed within two weeks. More commonly, the fixation devices remain under the skin and absorb over about one year.

Bathing and Hair Care

Patients are usually allowed to shower between three to seven days postoperative and, in some cases, as soon as the bandage is removed.

Shampooing, hair care, and gentle brushing can resume as early as the third postoperative day; however, due to temporary numbness in the scalp and the risk of a burn, a hair dryer (if used) should be set at medium-to-cool heat.

No hair coloring or stripping should be performed until cleared by the surgeon. Assuming the wounds have been reepithelialized, this is usually allowed after the third week postoperative.

Makeup

During the recovery period, the use of makeup and hairstyling is often used to cover minor bruising and swelling. If only the forehead-lift was done, makeup can usually be applied the following day, taking care not to get any on the suture line. If a blepharoplasty or face-lift was also done, please refer to the appropriate section in this book.

Sun Protection

It is important to avoid unprotected, direct sun exposure for several months after facial surgery. If patients must be outdoors for prolonged periods of time, it is recommended that they wear hats and sunscreen lotions with an SPF of 15 or greater, and high-quality sunglasses with UV filters should be worn.

POSTPROCEDURE SKIN/TISSUE CHANGES

The immediate postoperative experience for a patient who has had a classic forehead-lift may differ significantly from a patient who has had the endoscopic procedure. The healing time depends on the type, difficulty, and extent of the procedure(s) performed and the final result will be affected by the patient's bone structure, ability to heal, age, and physical condition.

Regardless of how tight the skin is pulled, acne scars, age spots, and fine lines will usually return to their original texture. Because the texture of the skin is not affected by a forehead-lift, skin-resurfacing procedures may be recommended as a "finishing touch" to improve the overall appearance of the facial skin.

For both procedures, visible signs of surgery usually fade completely within two to three weeks, and normal hair growth should return.

Although the surgeon may prescribe pain medication, there is usually little pain discomfort after a forehead-lift.

Classic Forehead-Lift

Patients will experience a certain amount of swelling and bruising in the immediate postoperative period. In some patients the cheek and eye area may be involved. These postoperative conditions are normal and usually begin to disappear seven to nine days postoperative. Patients may experience numbness on the scalp, which may be replaced by itching. These sensations may last for several months.

Although permanent hair loss is rare, some of the hair around the incision may fall out or may temporarily be thinner; however, normal hair growth will usually resume within a few weeks or months.

Endoscopic Forehead-Lift

Although this technique may require more surgery time, it is less invasive, producing less swelling, less itching, and less pain. Thus, compared with patients who have had the classic forehead-lift, those undergoing the endoscopic forehead-lift have a shorter recovery period. Regardless of the forehead-lift technique used, the results of a forehead-lift generally last 5 to 10 years. However, many patients enjoy permanent results.

Scars

The resulting scar(s) is/are camouflaged because they are either placed within the hairline or at the border of the hairline. If the incision was placed within a deep furrow of a frown line, the casual observer will perceive it as a natural wrinkle.

POSTPROCEDURE ACTIVITIES

To keep the swelling down, patients should keep their head elevated when lying down or sleeping for several days after surgery. In addition, cold compresses may be used in some patients to further reduce swelling. Most of the visible signs of surgery should fade completely within about three weeks. In general, patients who have had the endoscopic forehead-lift may feel ready to resume activities even sooner.

As with any surgery, patients may feel fatigued for some time after their procedure; although they should be up and about in a day or two, they should plan on taking it easy for at least the first week after surgery. Their energy level should slowly return as they begin to feel and look better.

Patients can expect to be at work and resume normal activities within seven to nine days. In many instances, patients will be able to resume most of their normal activities within two weeks and begin to exercise three to four weeks after surgery; however, rigorous activity should be avoided until cleared by their surgeon (e.g., activity that increases blood pressure, such as straining, bending, lifting, and sports activity).

SOME RISKS AND POSSIBLE COMPLICATIONS

Complications are rare and usually minor when a forehead-lift is performed by a qualified plastic surgeon. However, the following risks are possible:

- Bleeding
- Infection
- Hair loss along the scar edges
- Visible scarring
- Temporary or permanent sensory loss along the incision line
- Motor nerve damage, resulting in the loss of the ability to raise the eyebrows and wrinkle the forehead

Chapter 13

Hair Transplants
Hair Restoration Surgery

■ Jeffrey S. Epstein, MD, FACS

The goal of surgical hair restoration is simple—to restore hair to areas of loss. The challenge is to recreate Mother Nature so that the results appear as natural as possible.

The theories that baldness is caused by frequent shampooing, poor circulation to the scalp, vitamin deficiencies, dandruff, and even excessive hat wearing have been disproved. Hair loss is primarily caused by genetics, with aging and changes in hormones advancing the process. It has been estimated that hair loss affects 50 percent of all men who are 50 and 70 percent of men who are 70, whereas in women, the incidence is approximately 20 percent. As a rule, the earlier hair loss begins, the more severe the baldness will become.

For men, heredity is the major factor in hair loss. Male pattern baldness consists of losing hair in certain patterns (e.g., a receding hairline, frontotemporal recessions, or thinning at the crown). In females, hormonal changes, such as those that occur in menopause or in genetically predisposed women, are mainly responsible for subtle thinning and loss of density all over the scalp. Accidents, burns, and disease can also trigger hair loss. In such cases, replacement surgery is considered a reconstructive procedure.

By definition, surgical hair restoration techniques use the patient's own existing hair, thus total baldness makes replacement surgery impossible. By removing hair from one part of the scalp (the donor region) and transplanting it into an area devoid of hair (the recipient region), the hair will continue to grow just like it did in the donor region. If selected from the proper area, this growth will continue for an individual's lifetime.

Although there are several surgical options in the treatment of hair loss, it is important to understand that patients will never have the coverage that they enjoyed before their hair loss. This is because there is only a finite supply of donor hair. Once exhausted there are no more hairs to transplant. A dense donor supply allows for a greater amount of coverage.

The younger the person, the more conservative the approach must be for hair restoration surgery because of the higher risk of continued hair loss. This progressive nature of hair loss must be anticipated for and explained to the patient. Furthermore, because the transplants are permanent, the hairline should be created to look age-appropriate for years to come.

In women, the goal should be to increase density in areas that will strategically provide the greatest appearance of coverage. As donor density is usually lower in women than in men, less impressive results are typical.

MECHANISM OF ACTION AND TARGET TISSUES

Hair Grafts

With hair transplant techniques, a single strip of healthy, hair-bearing scalp is harvested from the sides and/or back of the scalp (Figure 13–1).

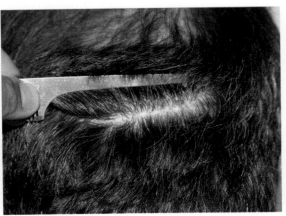

A

B

Figure 13–1

A, Closure of the donor site after harvesting a strip of donor hair. B, Same patient after donor site has healed.
Reprinted with permission of Jeffrey S. Epstein, MD, FACS. All rights reserved.

Figure 13–2

Surgical dissection of a strip of donor scalp into individual hair grafts.

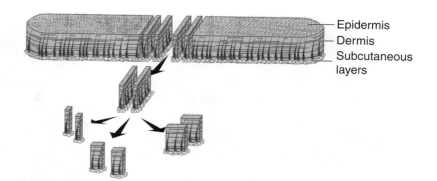

Epidermis
Dermis
Subcutaneous layers

This strip is then cut into small grafts and transplanted into the areas of baldness (Figure 13–2).

The original hair transplant techniques, as founded in the 1950s, used punch grafts—circular **plugs** of scalp containing 10 to 20 hairs per plug. The goal was to establish a "wall" of hair by placing these plug grafts next to each other over 2 to 4 sessions. Unaesthetic results were typical with these plugs.

The evolution of hair grafting has been toward the use of smaller and smaller grafts. **Minigrafts** consist of three to six hairs, whereas **micrografts** contain one or two hairs. Although the micrografting/minigrafting technique is still largely in use these days and capable of creating reasonably aesthetic results, a superior technique—**follicular unit grafting**—has taken its place as the gold standard. The more refined technique of follicular unit grafting differs from micro/minigrafting in that every graft consists of one to no more than four hairs, and these grafts are dissected out under a microscope for greater accuracy.

The transplanted hair goes into a temporary resting phase and then reappears within three months. Hair usually grows at about a half-inch per month. Once present, these grafts continue to grow hair on a permanent basis.

Scalp Flap

This procedure can quickly cover large areas of baldness by cutting, repositioning, and suturing a flap (peninsula) of the hair-bearing scalp into the defect left by the excision of the bald area. The scalp flap remains "tethered" to its original blood supply for uninterrupted circulation. The size of the flap and its placement is largely dependent on the patient's goals and needs.

Unlike small hair grafts, there is no temporary hair loss with scalp flaps. Thus, the resulting hairline is immediate. The hair continues to grow, in its new location, at the same rate of growth as in the previous location.

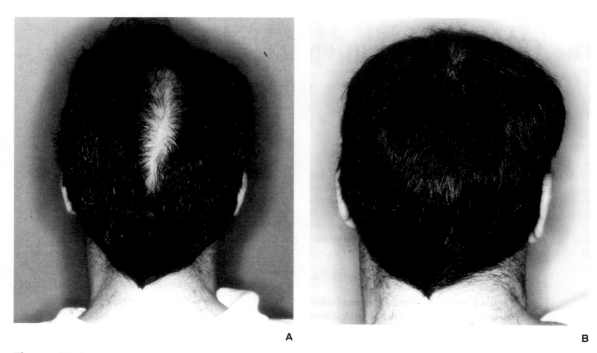

A **B**

Figure 13–3

A, Patient before scalp reduction. B, Same patient after a scalp reduction procedure. Reprinted with permission from *The American Journal of Cosmetic Surgery.*

Due to significant improvements in hair grafting techniques, scalp flaps are rarely performed today.

Scalp Reduction

This method can reduce or even completely eliminate the bald area of the crown and/or mid-scalp so that less hair grafts are required to attain the desired result (Figure 13–3). The bald scalp is excised, then the adjacent hair-bearing scalp tissue is stretched and the resulting scalp margins are sutured together.

As with scalp flaps, scalp reductions are largely of historical relevance, due to the risk of scarring and creation of abnormal hair-growth patterns.

Tissue Expanders

A **tissue expander** (a balloon-like device), which is attached to an injection port via a silicone tube, is implanted beneath the hair-bearing scalp that is adjacent to a bald area. Over a period of weeks to months,

Figure 13–4

Examples of tissue expanders. Reprinted with permission from Inamed Aesthetics.

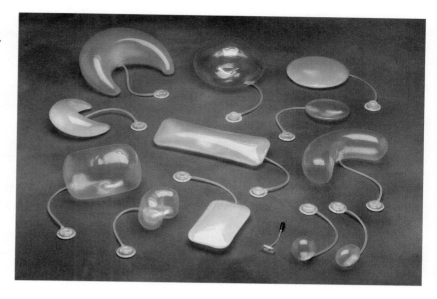

saline is injected into the injection port so that the balloon slowly expands the overlying scalp—much like the effects of pregnancy. These expanders come in all sizes and shapes (Figure 13–4).

Once the desired amount of excess scalp is obtained, another procedure is performed to remove the expander, excise the bald spot, and cover the resulting scalp defect with the adjacent (stretched) scalp. The healthy scalp margins are then sutured.

This technique is primarily applied to areas of scalp scarring, such as with burns.

PREPROCEDURE CONSIDERATIONS

Hair replacement surgery is an individualized treatment. The key factor in hair restoration surgery is the presence of suitable donor hair on the sides and/or back of the scalp. Aside from the artistic and technical capabilities of the surgeon, factors that affect the cosmetic outcome include hair quality, hair color, texture, and curliness. Gray or curly hair tends to make it easier to achieve density, whereas darker hair is more challenging to achieve undetectable.

Anesthesia

Most hair transplants are performed under local anesthesia with a sedative to relax the patient. Although patients may feel some tugging, they should not feel any pain.

General anesthesia may be used for more complex cases involving tissue expansion or flaps. Patients will then sleep through the procedure.

PROCEDURE/TECHNIQUE

Cosmetic hair replacement surgery is usually performed in a physician's office-based facility. Unlike extensive reconstructive hair restoration surgery, cosmetic hair restoration does not require a hospital stay.

As discussed earlier, there are a number of techniques used in hair replacement surgery. These include hair grafts, scalp flaps, scalp reduction, and tissue expanders. Yet, more than 99 percent of all hair restoration procedures performed are hair grafting.

Hair Grafts

Just before surgery, the hair in the *donor area* is trimmed short so that the grafts can be easily harvested. Typically, a strip of hair-bearing scalp is excised from the donor area and then (using a microscope for greater accuracy) the hair strip is dissected into several hundred to several thousand grafts, each containing one to four hairs. The grafts are then transplanted into tiny slits within the bald area. The donor site is closed with sutures.

With all hair grafting techniques, to ensure that the hair will grow in a natural direction, the grafts are typically placed facing forward. A transplant procedure takes between three to five hours, depending on the number of grafts. Some patients desire a second procedure to achieve additional density or wider area of coverage. A healing interval of six to eight months is usually recommended between procedures. With a second procedure, the original donor site scar is excised as part of the new donor strip.

The proper design and placement of the hairline is equally as important as the surgeon's skill in harvesting and placing each graft (Figure 13–5).

Scalp Flap

The scalp flap is dissected, taking care to maintain its blood supply. It is positioned into the desired area and sutured to the adjacent scalp. As with scalp reduction and tissue expanders, several procedures are usually necessary to correct significant baldness. The resulting scar is camouflaged, or at least obscured, by the relocated hair, which grows to the very edge of the incision.

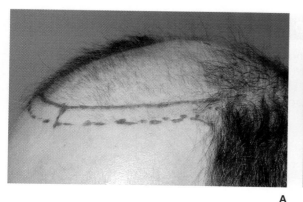 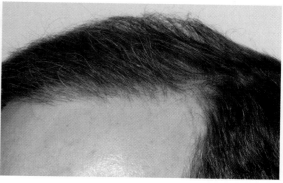

A

B

Figure 13–5

A, Design of proposed hairline. B, Same patient postoperative. Reprinted with permission of Jeffrey S. Epstein, MD, FACS. All rights reserved.

The size of the flap and its placement are largely dependent on the patient's needs and goals.

Scalp Reduction

This technique is sometimes referred to as **advancement flap surgery** because after the bald spot has been excised, sections of adjacent hair-bearing scalp are pulled forward (advanced) to fill in the bald area. Even after several procedures, complete removal of the bald area may not be achieved.

Tissue Expander

This technique yields dramatic results with significant coverage in a relatively short time. A balloon-like device (tissue expander) is inserted beneath hair-bearing scalp that lies adjacent to the bald or scarred area. The device is gradually inflated with saline over a period of weeks to months, causing the skin to expand. When the skin beneath the hair has stretched enough (usually about two months), another procedure is performed to remove the expander, excise the bald spot or scar, and rearrange and suture the margins of the adjacent tissue that was expanded.

With scalp flap, scalp reduction, or tissue expansion technique, most patients may need a surgical *touch-up* procedure to create more natural-looking results after their incisions have healed. Sometimes this involves blending, a filling-in of the hairline using a combination of hair grafts.

DRESSINGS AND WOUND CARE

After a hair graft procedure, the scalp is cleansed and no bandages are applied. Patients are instructed to keep their head elevated for two days postoperative. Hair washing may be resumed on the second day and a return to full activities at five days.

Sutures

Sutures are usually removed 8 to 10 days postoperative. Antibiotics are given for the first few days, and any discomfort or pain is controlled with oral medication.

Bathing and Hair Care

Patients may usually gently shampoo their hair by the second postoperative day. Very gentle towel drying is allowed and, if used, blow-dryers should be set on low heat.

Makeup

So long as care is taken to protect the scalp wounds and suture lines, makeup can resume the morning after surgery.

POSTPROCEDURE SKIN/TISSUE CHANGES

The newly transplanted hair normally falls out within 3 weeks after the procedure, and new hair reappears within 12 weeks postoperative.

Scars

In the place of the donor site, a fine straight-line scar will result. The scar is usually 2-mm wide and is easily camouflaged and/or obscured by adjacent hair, which grows to the very edge of the incision. Wide scars, due to "stretch-back" (caused by tension), may result from some procedures. The individual graft will form a small crust and will ultimately heal with no visible scar (Figure 13–6).

POSTPROCEDURE ACTIVITIES

How soon patients resume their normal routine depends on the length, complexity, and type of hair restoration. Patients should plan

Figure 13–6

Appearance of scalp one day postoperative in a patient with thinning hair who received hair grafts. Reprinted with permission of Jeffrey S. Epstein, MD, FACS. All rights reserved.

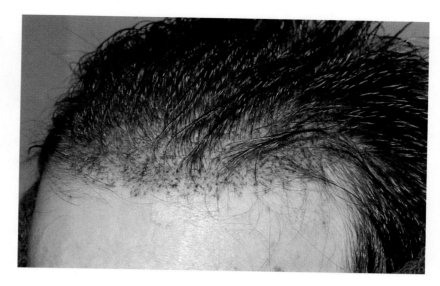

to take it easy for a day or two after the procedure. Most patients may feel well enough to go back to work and resume normal, light activity several days postoperatively. Because strenuous activity increases blood flow to the scalp and may cause bleeding, patients are instructed to avoid vigorous exercise and contact sports for up to five days, when full activities can resume. (For examples of preoperative and postoperative results see Figures 13–7, 13–8, and 13–9.)

SOME RISKS AND POSSIBLE COMPLICATIONS

Hair replacement surgery is a procedure with a low rate of complications when performed by a qualified, experienced physician. Risks, however, can include:

- Superficial infection
- Bleeding
- Flap loss and/or full thickness scalp loss with scalp flaps or reductions
- Shock loss—damage to surrounding hairs

Figure 13–7

Preoperative and postoperative patient with thinning hair. Reprinted with permission of Jeffrey S. Epstein, MD, FACS. All rights reserved.

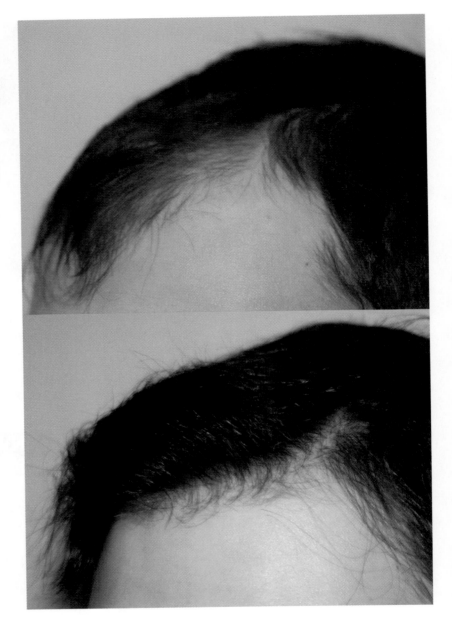

Figure 13–8

Another preoperative and postoperative patient with thinning hair. Reprinted with permission of Jeffrey S. Epstein, MD, FACS. All rights reserved.

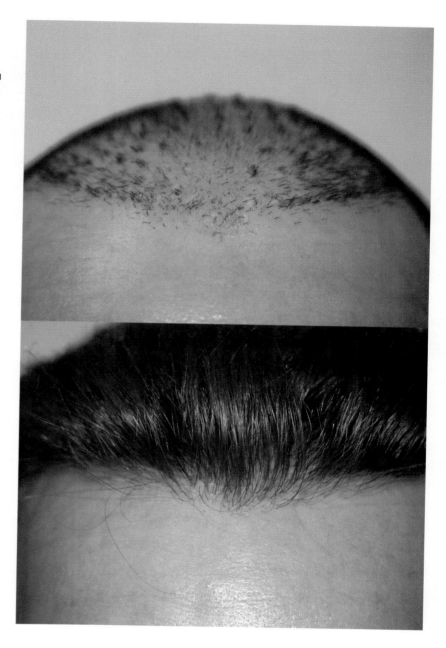

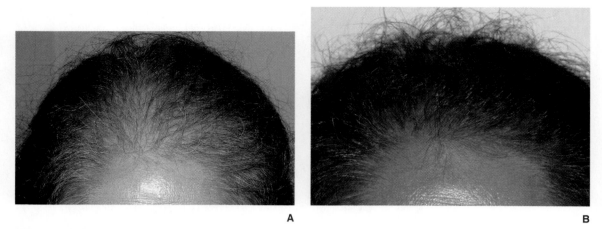

Figure 13–9

A, Female patient with thinning hair. B, Same patient postoperative. Reprinted with permission of Jeffrey S. Epstein, MD, FACS. All rights reserved.

Chapter 14

Eye-Lift Blepharoplasty

■ Alan Matarasso, MD

Blepharoplasty is one of the most often performed cosmetic surgical procedures. In 2003, the American Society of Aesthetic Plastic Surgeons reported more than 260,000 blepharoplasty procedures. It can be done alone or in conjunction with a face-lift, brow-lift, or other cosmetic procedures.

Factors that may contribute to baggy upper eyelids and bulging lower eyelids include genetics, aging, lifestyle issues, and/or the damaging effects of the sun.

INDICATIONS

The best candidates for a cosmetic blepharoplasty are usually men and women with redundant skin in the upper eyelids and/or baggy lower eyelids.

Blepharoplasty cannot alter dark circles, fine lines, or wrinkles around the eyes, nor can it change sagging eyebrows. For sagging eyebrows a lift in the temple region will elevate the heavy overhang of the eyebrow.

MECHANISM OF ACTION AND TARGET TISSUES

Redundant eyelid skin is excised. If needed, a strip of **orbicularis oculi muscle** (Figure 4–1) is also excised along with the upper eyelid skin. If bulging exists, some **periorbital fat** is excised.

Figure 14–1

External incision for upper and lower blepharoplasty.

PREPROCEDURE CONSIDERATIONS

Typically, a history and physical examination is done to evaluate the patient's general health. A visual field test and/or assessment of tear production may also be performed. The physician will assess the patient's eyelids to determine the tissues that need to be addressed and whether any additional procedures are appropriate (e.g., laser resurfacing or brow-lift).

A few medical conditions make blepharoplasty more risky (e.g., thyroid problems such as hypothyroidism and **Graves' disease** and lack of sufficient tears).

Anesthesia

Blepharoplasty is usually performed using local anesthesia with intravenous sedation or a systemic anesthesia, which makes the patient feel drowsy and relaxed; however, the patient may feel some tugging or occasional discomfort as the periorbital fat is removed. The anesthesia is usually mixed with adrenaline, which causes **vasoconstriction** to minimize the bleeding in the surgical field. General anesthesia may also be used.

PROCEDURE/TECHNIQUE

A blepharoplasty may be performed in a surgeon's office-based facility, an outpatient surgery center, or in a hospital.

After induction of anesthesia, the patient is prepped and draped in a sterile fashion. For both *upper and lower eyelid blepharoplasty,* the incisions are placed on, adjacent to, or parallel to the patient's natural lines and creases around the eyes. The incision may be extended to the crow's feet lines on the outer corners of the eye to minimize appearance of the resulting scars (Figure 14–1).

Figure 14–2

Upper eyelid incisions.

In the *upper eyelids,* a long, elliptical island of skin is excised, with or without muscle. Through this incision, excess fat is removed (Figure 14–2).

In the *lower lids,* the skin flap is dissected and, if needed, excess **periorbital fat** is excised (Figure 14–3). After *hemostasis* is attained with **electrocautery**, the skin is trimmed of excess skin and muscle, sutured with fine nonabsorbable sutures, and covered with steri-strips.

In situations where there are bulging pockets of fat beneath the lower eyelids but no skin redundancy, the surgeon may perform a **transconjunctival blepharoplasty** where *the incision is made inside* the **(conjunctiva)** lower eyelid, leaving no visible external scar (Figure 14–4). This is usually performed on younger patients with thicker, more elastic skin. The periorbital fat is excised and the conjunctiva can be closed with a special suturing technique.

Together, upper and lower blepharoplasty usually takes 45 minutes to 2 hours, depending on the extent of the surgery. If done separately, each procedure will take less time.

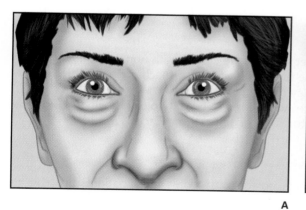

A

B

Figure 14–3

A, Baggy lower eyelids. B, Same patient after lower blepharoplasty.

Figure 14–4

Transconjunctival incision.

If there are excess wrinkles below the eyes, a laser resurfacing can be performed simultaneously.

DRESSINGS AND WOUND CARE

Typically, the eyes are not usually bandaged after surgery. Rather, the surgeon may lubricate the eyelids with ointment and place ice compresses over the eyes while the patient is in the reclined position.

As the anesthesia wears off, the eyelids may feel tight and sore. If this occurs, the patient should respond well to over-the-counter pain medications. If the pain is severe, the surgeon must be notified immediately. Patients may also experience excessive tearing and light sensitivity (**photophobia**) for several weeks postoperative. Many surgeons recommend the use of eye drops for patients who experience dryness, burning, or itching.

Sutures

The upper and lower wounds are closed with nonabsorbable sutures. If the incision for the *transconjunctival* approach is closed with fine absorbable sutures, they can be left in place.

Permanent sutures will be removed in two to five days postoperative. Absorbable sutures are usually left in place.

Bathing and Hair Care

By the third or fourth postoperative day, most patients are able to shower and gently wash their face and hair with mild soap/shampoo. The eyes should not be rubbed for several weeks postoperative. Hair coloring should not be done until the surgical wound is completely healed/epithelialized.

Makeup

By 7 to 10 days, depending on the patient's rate of healing and the doctor's preferences, the patient will probably be able to wear makeup to hide the bruising that remains. Other facial and eyelid makeup, including mascara, eye shadow, eyeliner, and artificial eyelashes, may be applied after the first week of surgery. When resuming application, including mascara, patients are generally instructed to use *new* eye makeup.

Upper Eyelids

Makeup should not be applied to the upper eyelids until the incision line is completely reepithelialized and dry—approximately seven days.

Lower Eyelids

Makeup may be gently applied onto the lower lids between four to six days postoperative, but care must be taken not to put any of the makeup in the incision line. Makeup should be gently removed at the end of each day.

Contact Lenses

Generally, contacts can be worn within the first 7 to 10 days postoperative, depending on the individual.

Sun Protection

It is important to avoid unprotected, direct sun exposure for several months after blepharoplasty surgery. If patients must be outdoors for prolonged periods of time, it is recommended that they wear hats and sunscreen lotions with an SPF of 15 or greater. High-quality sunglasses with UV filters should also be worn.

POSTPROCEDURE SKIN/TISSUE CHANGES

A certain degree of swelling is expected after a blepharoplasty, and bruising varies from person to person. Both *edema* and *ecchymosis* will reach their peak during the first week and generally last anywhere from two to six weeks. There may also be temporary swelling of the conjunctiva or at the corner of the eyelids. Shortly after, the edema and discoloration around the eyes will gradually subside, and the patient will start to look and feel much better.

Occasionally, tiny whiteheads *(milia)* may appear after the stitches are taken out. The surgeon can easily remove these.

Scars

Typically, because of the strategic placement of the incisions, scarring is minimal and usually unnoticeable to the casual observer. However, healing is a gradual process. Scars may occasionally remain slightly pink for six months or more after surgery. Eventually, they will fade to a thin, nearly invisible scar.

POSTPROCEDURE ACTIVITIES

Most patients return home the same day. However, medication used during the procedure may cause blurred vision for several hours. This, along with ointment in the eyes and/or dressings over the eyes, makes it necessary for patients to have assistance for one to two days postoperative. Driving should not resume until cleared by the surgeon.

Patients should keep their activities to a minimum for 3 to 5 days and avoid strenuous activities that raise blood pressure, such as bending, lifting, and rigorous sports, for about 3 weeks. It is especially important to avoid strenuous activities. Patients should be able to read or watch television by the second or third day postoperative. Most patients are ready to go out in public and/or back to work in 7 to 10 days.

SOME RISKS AND POSSIBLE COMPLICATIONS

The following are some possible risks that can occur with eye-lifts:

- Double (**diplopia**) or blurred vision for a few days postoperative
- Lagophthalmos—difficulty closing eyes completely
- **Ectropion**—a pulling down of the lower lids
- Slight asymmetry in healing
- **Dry eye**
- Scarring and pigmentary changes of the suture line
- Cysts and suture tunnels
- Infection
- Bleeding/hematoma
- Photophobia—light sensitivity
- Ptosis—sagging of the upper eyelids
- Blindness

Chapter 15

Nose Jobs
Rhinoplasty

Joel M. Levin, MD, FACS

Rhinoplasty, commonly known as a nose job, is one of the most common aesthetic procedures. It is a very delicate operation requiring specialized training and experience. Most rhinoplasty procedures are performed for cosmetic reasons. When a rhinoplasty is done to relieve nasal airway obstruction, it is called **reconstructive rhinoplasty**, which can be done alone or in conjunction with a **cosmetic rhinoplasty**, if warranted. Although complex procedures may require a short hospital stay, most patients return home the same day.

INDICATIONS

The goal of a cosmetic rhinoplasty is to create harmony between the nose and other facial features. Rhinoplasty can reduce or increase the size of the nose, change the shape of the tip, change the shape of the bridge, narrow the span of the nostrils, or change the angle between the nose and the upper lip. Rhinoplasty is often performed with chin and/or cheek implants.

Although there is no upper age limit for cosmetic nasal surgery, most surgeons prefer to delay operating on younger patients until they have completed their growth spurts, which is usually in the mid-teens for girls and the mid- to late-teens for boys.

Deviated nasal septum and/or **enlarged nasal turbinates** can contribute to nasal airway obstruction and are repaired (reconstructive rhinoplasty) respectively via a septoplasty and/or turbinectomy.

135

MECHANISM OF ACTION AND TARGET TISSUES

Through strategically placed incisions, the main structural support (nasal bones, septum, and alar cartilages) for the nose is exposed. They are then fractured, sculpted, and trimmed to attain the desired size and shape. Upon completion, the skin and mucosa are redraped and closed with key sutures (Figure 15–1).

PREPROCEDURE CONSIDERATIONS

Factors that can influence the procedure and results include the structure of the nasal bones, the support cartilage at the tip of the nose, the shape of the septum, the shape of the face, the thickness of the skin, and even the patient's age and race. Menstruation may affect intraoperative and postoperative bleeding.

Anesthesia

Depending on the extent of the procedure and the patient's and/or surgeon's preference, rhinoplasty can be performed under local or general anesthesia. The local anesthetic solution contains adrenaline, which is a vasoconstrictor that temporarily reduces the blood flow to the surgical area. With local anesthesia the patient is awake but lightly sedated.

PROCEDURE/TECHNIQUES

There are two surgical techniques for performing rhinoplasty: the **endonasal** approach, commonly known as a **closed rhinoplasty** and the **open rhinoplasty**. Through strategically placed incisions, both techniques allow access to the nose's framework of bone and cartilage. The major part of the incisions in either the "closed" or "open" rhinoplasties are within the nasal cavity to avoid visible scarring (Figure 15–2).

The framework is exposed and sculpted to create the desired shape (e.g., the nasal hump and septal cartilage may be trimmed to reduce the profile of the nose and/or to elevate the tip of the nose [Figure 15–3]). In some cases, a synthetic implant or cartilage from another part of the body may be added to obtain the nose's ultimate shape. The sides of the nasal bones—where they meet the cheeks and bridge of the nose—are fractured, or sawed (Figure 15–4), and the loose nasal bones are then compressed together to form a new shape. Total surgery time depends

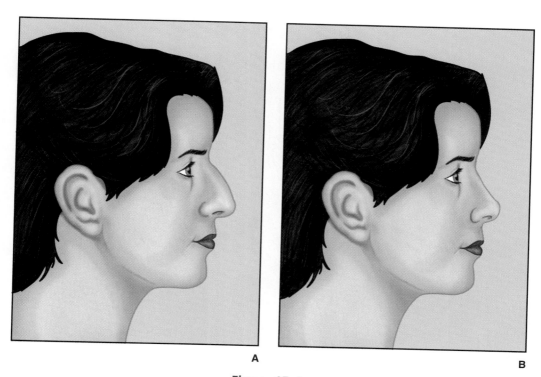

Figure 15–1
A, Patient with prominent nasal hump. B, Same patient after a cosmetic rhinoplasty.

Figure 15–2
Incision placed within the nostril.

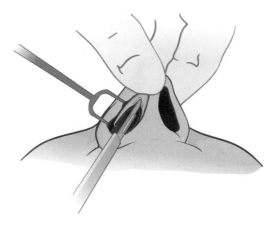

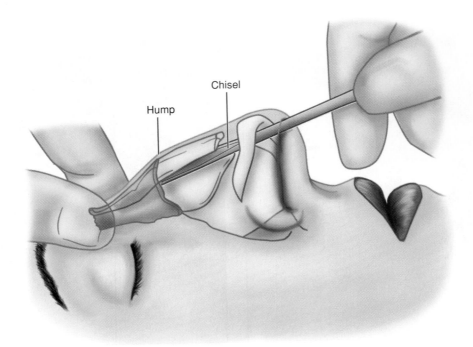

Figure 15–3
Removing the hump of the nose.

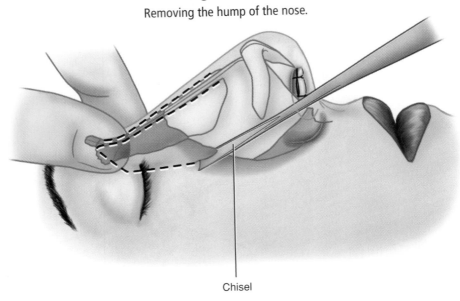

Figure 15–4
Fracturing the lateral nasal walls.

on the type, difficulty, the surgeon's experience, and scope of the procedure(s) performed. Typically, this procedure usually takes one to one and a half hours to complete. Additional procedures, such as a septoplasty, a turbinectomy, or facial implants, will lengthen the surgery time.

When the surgeon is satisfied with the resulting changes in the bone and cartilaginous framework, the tissues are then redraped over the new frame and the wound margins are sutured.

"Closed" Rhinoplasty

With *closed rhinoplasty,* all of the incisions are made within the cavity of the nostrils and nasal airway, allowing the surgery to be performed entirely within the nose, thus avoiding external scars.

"Open" Rhinoplasty

The *open rhinoplasty* technique may be used in more complicated cases (or as the surgeon's preference), because the skeletal and cartilaginous framework is better visualized. The incisions are basically the same as with the "closed" rhinoplasty; however, a small transverse incision is made across the outer skin of the **columella**, the bridge between the nostrils (Figure 15–5).

Alar Resection

Patients wishing to diminish flared (**alar**) nostrils require a **wedge excision** at the lateral aspect of both nostrils. These incisions are placed in the skin's natural creases to make them as inconspicuous as possible (Figure 15–6). Thus, like the resulting transverse scar on the *columella* used in open rhinoplasty they usually go unnoticed by the casual observer.

> **Septoplasty**—the surgical manipulation and contouring of the nasal septum (cartilage that divides the inside of the nose) to correct breathing problems.
>
> **Turbinectomy**—the surgical reduction of the size of the turbinates (tissue along the lateral wall of the nasal wall) to correct breathing problems.

Figure 15–5

Transverse incision to the columella.

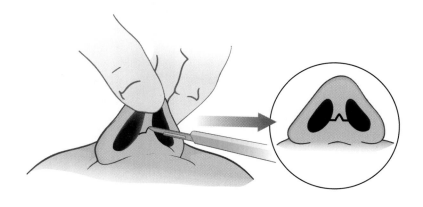

Figure 15–6

Lateral wedge resection.

DRESSINGS AND WOUND CARE

At the end of the procedure, lubricated packing strips may be inserted into both nostrils. A protective splint is then secured over the nose to protect it and help maintain its new shape (Figure 15–7). A drip pad is taped to cover the nostrils to collect postoperative oozing; it is changed as needed. Using cold compresses and keeping the head elevated will help reduce swelling, bruising, and sooth the patient. If

Figure 15–7

Nasal splint. Reprinted with permission from Shippert Medical and Design Veronique.

lubricated packing strips were placed inside the nose after surgery, they are removed the following morning. The external splint can usually be removed after seven days.

Shortly after surgery, the patient may experience slight pain around the surgical area, and some may experience a dull headache. The most common immediate postoperative experience is a small amount of bleeding from the nostrils, which typically stops in one or two hours; patients may continue to feel some nasal stuffiness for several weeks. During this period, patients should avoid blowing their nose. Prescription glasses can be taped to the forehead until the nose is completely healed.

Sutures

Absorbable stitches (sutures) are used to close the incision within the nostrils. Nonabsorbable stitches are used if external incisions were used (e.g., the skin of the columella and/or nostril). Any stitches outside of the nostrils will be removed in five to seven days. Stitches placed within the nostrils usually do not need to be removed because they are absorbed.

Bathing and Hair Care

Bathing and washing the hair can be done within two to three days after surgery. Again, extreme care should be taken to avoid touching the nose.

Makeup

Camouflage cosmetics can be applied gently after the nasal splint is removed to cover the discoloration after the first day or two.

Sun Protection

Avoid unprotected sun exposure for eight weeks postoperative.

POSTPROCEDURE SKIN/TISSUE CHANGES

Healing is a gradual process. Swelling and bruising of the nose and around the eyes is common after surgery and will subside after the first week or two. Some subtle swelling, unnoticeable to anyone but the patient and the surgeon, will remain for several months. Breathing through the nose may be difficult for the first few days

Avoid Touching the Nose for Several Months after Surgery

It usually takes several months after surgery for the fractured nasal bones to heal properly. Therefore, even with a nasal splint in place, pressure to the nose must be avoided because the healing bones can shift, resulting in a deformity. This is important to understand when considering postoperative activity, including bathing, massages, hair care, and routine activities.

postoperative, but it will improve as the internal swelling subsides. After surgery, small "burst" blood vessels may appear as tiny red spots on the skin's surface; these are usually minor but may be permanent.

Scars

Obvious or *hypertrophic scars* are extremely rare because most of the incisions are within the nostrils. Even when the *columella* is incised with a scalpel in the "open" technique, or when "wedge resections" are removed from the outer nostrils, the scars are usually not visible because the incisions are strategically placed to fool the eye of the casual observer.

POSTPROCEDURE ACTIVITIES

Each patient is different, and the complexity of the surgery varies from patient to patient. In general, the patient should rest with the head elevated for the first 12 to 24 hours after surgery. Most rhinoplasty patients are up and about within 2 days. Typically patients can resume normal activities within 5 to 7 days, including school and sedentary work.

In general, patients should avoid strenuous activity the first three weeks postoperative; avoid activity that places the face in potential danger of trauma; avoid rubbing the nose; and avoid unprotected sun exposure for eight weeks. Sneezing should be done through the mouth.

SOME RISKS AND POSSIBLE COMPLICATIONS

In the hands of qualified cosmetic surgeons, complications are *infrequent* and usually minor. Nevertheless, there is always the possibility of complications, including:

- Infection
- Bleeding
- Reaction to the anesthesia
- Asymmetry
- Small "burst" blood vessels may appear as tiny red spots on the skin's surface

Chapter 16

Facial Implants

Facial implants are designed for augmentation, reconstruction, or rejuvenation of the face. They have been used for more than 20 years to improve and/or enhance facial contours and provide harmony and balance to the face. This chapter will focus on the most common facial implants: cheek, nose, and chin.

INDICATIONS

If the projection of the chin is weak or receding, it makes the nose look larger than it really is and fatty necks become more acute. Because loss of chin projection may occur with aging, adding a *chin implant* (**mentoplasty**) at the time of a face-lift or a rhinoplasty can improve the neck contour, profile, and jaw line in these patients. *Cheek implants* correct flatness in the mid-face by increasing the projection of the cheekbones, which serves to rejuvenate the mid-face region. *Nasal implants* are used to better define or add projection to the dorsum of the nose.

Facial implants are often combined with other facial cosmetic procedures such as rhinoplasty, face-lift, and/or *submental* liposuction.

MECHANISM OF ACTION AND TARGET TISSUES

Facial implants come in a variety of synthetic, solid, and semisolid materials, sizes, and styles for the chin, cheek, nose, and jaw. Small synthetic implants are inserted between soft tissue and bone over the desired area. After healing, the skin drapes smoothly over the implants, conforming to the bone, and the implants are usually undetectable. By virtue of its physical properties, the desired area is augmented (i.e., high cheekbones and/or a better-defined chin, which is especially apparent in the profile). The results are essentially permanent.

PREPROCEDURE CONSIDERATIONS

Patients with gum or dental problems may not be candidates for placement of facial implants via the intraoral route. Smoking inhibits blood flow to the skin and may delay the healing process of the incisions.

Anesthesia

Facial implant surgery may be done with either local anesthesia combined with a sedative, or general anesthesia.

PROCEDURE/TECHNIQUES

Surgery usually takes place in an office-based facility, a free-standing surgical center, or a hospital outpatient facility. The procedure follows a similar pattern for all facial areas.

Chin

An incision is made either in the natural (external) crease line just under the chin or (internal) inside the mouth, where gum and lower lip meet. A pocket is created between the bone and soft tissue, the implant is inserted, and the incision is sutured. During the procedure, the surgeon selects the proper size and shape implant for the patient. Insertion of a chin implant may take anywhere from 30 minutes to 1 hour (Figure 16–1).

Nose

The dorsum of the nose can be enhanced with synthetic implants placed as a sole procedure or in conjunction with a cosmetic or reconstructive rhinoplasty. The implants may be inserted through the incisions made for those procedures.

Figure 16–1

A, Weak chin. B, After a chin implant.

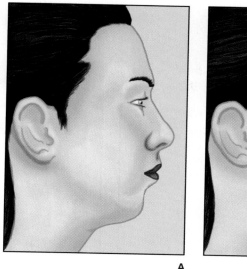
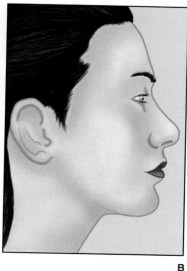

A   B

Cheek

When cheek implants are being placed in conjunction with another cosmetic procedure, such as a face-lift, forehead-lift, or eyelid surgery, the implants may be inserted through the incisions made for those procedures.

If the cheek implant is performed separately, two small *incisions* (Figure 16–2) will be made inside the upper lip, directly below the cheekbones. A pocket is created between the bone and soft tissue, the implant is inserted, and the incision is sutured. Each implant will be

Figure 16–2

Intraoral incision for cheek implants. Reprinted with permission from *The American Journal of Cosmetic Surgery.*

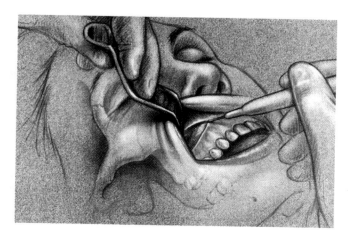

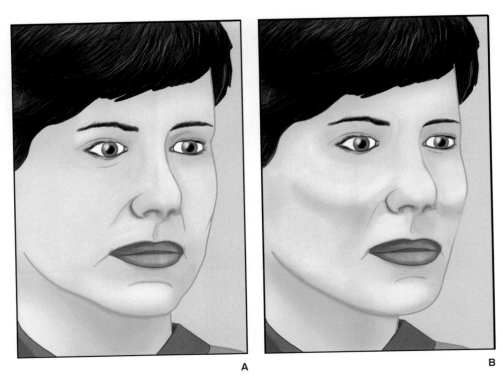

Figure 16–3

A, Flat mid-face. B, After a cheek implant.

fitted between the soft tissue of the cheek, under the *periosteum* of the cheekbone. After the implants are solidly in place, the incisions are closed using absorbable sutures (stitches). This procedure usually takes one to two hours (Figure 16–3).

DRESSINGS AND WOUND CARE

Upon completion of the implant surgery, a dressing or tape will be applied to assist in securing the implant(s) and minimize discomfort and swelling. If used, this tape will be removed in two to three days.

Postoperative bruising and swelling is a mild/moderate discomfort for one to two days. Mild discomfort is usually controlled with medications. The instructions, severity, and duration of side effects may vary, particularly if another cosmetic procedure is performed at the same time.

Sutures

If external sutures were used, they are removed in 5 to 10 days. If an intraoral incision was used, the sutures are allowed to dissolve over time.

Bathing and Hair Care

If the implants were introduced into the pocket via incision in the mouth, patients are given special instructions regarding oral hygiene. The face can be gently washed, taking care to avoid any pressure on the implant surgery area.

Makeup

If an intraoral incision was used to place the implant, camouflage cosmetics can be applied gently. If the implant was inserted via an external approach, care must be taken not to get any into the healing incisions.

POSTPROCEDURE SKIN/TISSUE CHANGES

There will be some discomfort and swelling around the surgical area but this usually subsides in about a week. Most patients with *facial implants* feel a stretched, tight sensation after the surgery. Black and blue marks may be visible around and below the surgical area. Surprisingly, with proper makeup, the casual observer may not even recognize that the patient has had a facial implant. After approximately six weeks, most swelling will be gone.

Most patients with *cheek* implants will temporarily have a diminished ability to move their mouth and lips, making it difficult to smile and talk much within the first few days. Some swelling and bruising can be expected and usually subsides within the first two weeks; however, the tissue will continue to settle for several weeks or months before the final result is attained.

A facial implant can *shift* slightly out of alignment and a second operation may be necessary to replace it in its proper position. Rarely, excess tightening and hardening of *scar* tissue around an implant can cause an unnatural shape. *Infection* or implant *rejection* is very *uncommon*, but if this occurs, the implant can easily be removed.

As with any surgical procedure, superficial sensory nerves may be interrupted and, consequently, the patient may have diminished sensation in the immediate area. Most sensory deficits are temporary, but some diminished feelings may last indefinitely. Facial (motor) nerve injury with weakness of a part of the face can occur on a transient or permanent basis; however, this is very rare.

Scars

When the incision is inside the mouth or inside the lower eyelid (conjunctiva), no scarring is visible to the casual observer.

POSTPROCEDURE ACTIVITIES

With either chin or cheek implants, most individuals return to their usual activities in 7 to 10 days. However, rigorous activity and rough contact to the implant area must be avoided for 4 to 6 weeks. Chewing will probably be limited immediately after *chin surgery*; patients with cheek implants will usually experience some temporary difficulty with smiling and talking. A liquid and/or soft food diet may be required for a few days after surgery. If the implant was placed intraoral, a soft diet and special oral hygiene will be prescribed until cleared by the surgeon.

SOME RISKS AND POSSIBLE COMPLICATIONS

The following are some risks that can occur with facial implants:

- Unnatural shape
- Infection
- Implant can shift slightly out of alignment
- Diminished sensation in the immediate area (temporary versus permanent)
- Facial (motor) nerve injury (temporary versus permanent)
- Implant exposure

Lip Implants
Thread-like synthetic material, like a *Gortex*, can be implanted into the lip(s) for added fullness. Implantation procedures for the lips are done with local or general anesthesia. A tiny incision is placed at either end of the lip, the implant is inserted, and the incisions are sutured.

Chin surgery, also known as *mentoplasty*, is a surgical procedure to reshape the chin either by enhancement with an implant or reduction surgery on the bone.

Some of the implant materials are made of a solid silicone. Contrary to popular belief, there is no scientific evidence that silicone (implants) is a harmful substance.

Chapter 17

Breast Implants
Augmentation Mammaplasty

■ Leslie H. Stevens, MD, FACS

Breast implants for augmentation, technically known as augmentation mammaplasty, uses **synthetic** implants to enhance the size and shape of a woman's breast.

> There is no evidence that breast implants will affect fertility, pregnancy, or ability to nurse.

Because gravity, pregnancy, and the effects of aging will eventually alter the size and shape of virtually every woman's breasts, it is not surprising that breast implant surgery is one of the most common cosmetic procedures sought by women in the United States.

INDICATIONS

Breast implants are used to enlarge and/or reshape women's breast(s) due to inherited small breast size, weight loss, childbirth, aging, tubular breast(s), and/or breast asymmetry. Breast implants can also be used to reconstruct breasts after a mastectomy for breast cancer.

MECHANISM OF ACTION AND TARGET TISSUES

A synthetic breast implant is positioned *behind the breast tissue only* or **pectoralis muscle** and breast tissue to increase projection and breast size, while achieving the most natural appearance possible.

There are a variety of implant designs, all of which have advantages and disadvantages. The implant used most often for augmentation purposes is made of a silicone envelope filled with saline (salt

149

In 1992, because of safety concerns, the Food and Drug Administration (FDA) restricted the use of silicone gel-filled implants to women willing to participate in long-term studies with specific indications for surgery.

water) solution via a detachable silicone tube that couples with a syringe—for filling the implant at the time of surgery.

The incision placement and positioning of the breast implant (relative to the pectoralis muscle) will depend on the patient's anatomy and the surgeon's recommendation and/or preference. One of the advantages of a saline implant is that it is filled with saline after it is inserted into a pocket through an approximately 4.0-cm incision facilitating its implantation.

If the breasts are sagging, a breast-lift (mastopexy) may be recommended in conjunction with the augmentation.

PREPROCEDURE CONSIDERATIONS

Patients who are planning to lose a significant amount of weight or planning a pregnancy might consider postponing breast implant surgery accordingly, because these events can alter breast size in an unpredictable manner. At the initial consultation, the surgeon will take a thorough medical history and inquire about any history of breast cancer and/or results of previous mammograms. A physical examination is then performed to determine whether the patient is a good candidate for breast implants. If so, the surgeon will explore breast enhancement options with the patient.

The size of the implant and the technique used will depend on the condition of the breasts, the body proportions, and the patient's expectations. Other options include incision placement, size and type of implant, and whether the implants will be placed beneath the pectoralis muscle or between the pectoralis muscle and the breast gland.

Mammograms and Breast Implants

Although there is no scientific evidence that breast implants cause breast cancer, they may change the way mammography is done to detect cancer. Technicians should be experienced in the special techniques required to get a reliable X-ray of a breast with an implant.

Although usually not necessary, it is not unreasonable to obtain a mammogram before breast implant surgery. It may pick up an early breast cancer and/or serve as a baseline mammogram to compare with future studies. In some instances, the surgeon may recommend another mammographic examination some months after surgery.

For women in the appropriate age group, routine mammograms should be continued after breast augmentation. Some women with a high risk for breast cancer may require additional breast diagnostics such as ultrasound or an *MRI*. However, the presence of breast implants makes it technically more difficult to take and read mammograms and could delay or hinder the early detection of breast cancer. As such, the technician should use special techniques to optimize the interpretation of the mammogram.

After breast augmentation, patients will still be able to perform breast self-examination.

Anesthesia

Breast augmentation is often performed using local anesthesia with a light intravenous sedation to make the patient feel drowsy and relaxed. General anesthesia may also be used, causing the patient to sleep during the procedure. The choice of anesthesia is made after considering the patient's wish/needs and the surgeon's preference.

PROCEDURE/TECHNIQUES

Most breast augmentations are performed on an outpatient basis, in the surgeon's office-based surgical suite, outpatient surgery center, or a hospital.

Placement of the Incisions

Several different incisions (Figure 17–1) are used for placement of the implants, all of which are designed to result in scarring that is usually

Figure 17–1

Possible incision sites. The umbilical incision site is not depicted here.

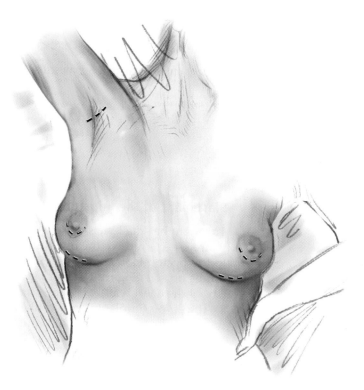

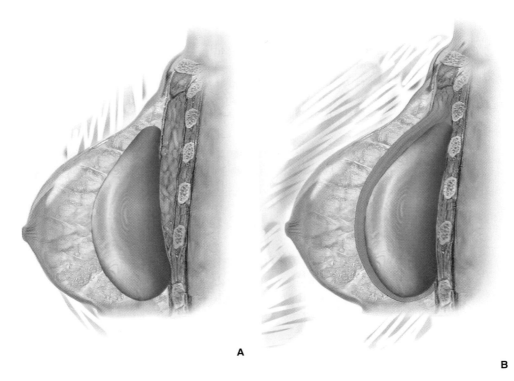

A

B

Figure 17–2

A, Subglandular placement of the implant. B, Submuscular placement of the implant.

unnoticed by the casual observer (e.g., the **inframammary crease** incision [where the breast meets the chest], the **circumareolar** incision [the outer margin of the dark skin surrounding the nipple], the axilla [armpit], or the transumbilical breast augmentation incision [belly button]).

Placement of the Implants

Through the small incision, the surgeon dissects a pocket in the chest wall tissue to receive the implant. This pocket will be created relative to the pectoralis muscle (i.e., either between the breast and the pectoralis muscle [Figure 17–2] or between the pectoralis muscle and the ribs of the chest wall).

The empty implant is rolled like a cigar and carefully inserted into the resulting pocket, such that the *injection tube* remains outside the incision for ease of inflation. A saline-filled syringe is then coupled to the silicone injection tube, and the implant is slowly inflated to the desired size. The inflated implant is then centered, and after the surgeon

Figure 17–3

Breast implant and inflation system. Reprinted with permission from Inamed Aesthetics.

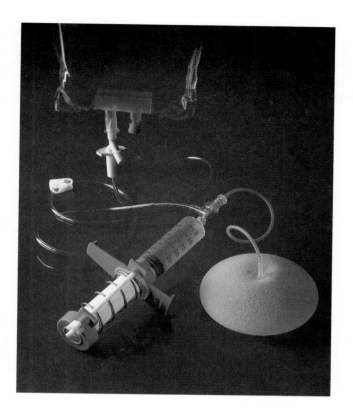

is satisfied with the symmetry and placement of the implant, the injection tube is gently pulled out from the self-sealing valve in the implant (Figure 17–3).

Some surgeons insert drainage tubes, which are removed several days after the surgery.

To avoid stitch marks and minimize the appearance of the surgical scar, the incision is closed in two layers: the deep layer is closed with interrupted, absorbable sutures and the superficial layer is closed with running, nonabsorbable subcuticular sutures. The incision is then covered with steri-strips and covered with absorbent pads. The patient is then either wrapped in an ace bandage or placed in a special bra to compress the breasts (Figure 17–4).

The length of the surgery usually takes one to two hours, depending on the technique, the placement of the implants, and the patient's anatomy, as well as the ancillary procedures performed (e.g., **mastopexy**).

Immediately after surgery, the patient is taken to the recovery room for further monitoring. When stable, most patients may be permitted to go home after a few hours.

Implant placement behind the pectoralis muscle may interfere less with a mammogram than if the implant is placed directly behind the breast tissue.

Figure 17–4

Surgical support bra. Reprinted with permission from Shippert Medical and Design Veronique.

Dressings and Wound Care

The surgeon may remove the dressings to check the incision area two to three days postoperative. If a drain was placed, the patient is instructed in caring and periodic draining of the fluid collection bulb, and it is usually removed in two to three days. At this point, the patient may be placed in a surgical support bra to wear for several weeks postoperative.

Sutures

The deep, interrupted, absorbable *subcuticular* sutures are left in place. The running, subcuticular sutures are removed 7 to 10 days postoperative, and the suture line is covered with a steri-strip and sterile dressing.

Bathing and Hair Care

Usually patients may be able to shower immediately if a waterproof dressing was applied. If the incision is closed and not draining, it can be gently washed with soap and water. The surgical incision should not be scrubbed with a washcloth for two to three weeks. Patients should not soak in a tub until the incision line is completely reepithelialized and there is no sign of drainage. The surgical area and incision should be gently blotted with a fresh clean towel.

Makeup

Patients can usually resume applying makeup the day after surgery.

POSTPROCEDURE SKIN/TISSUE CHANGES

For the first few days postoperative, patients with the breast implant placed behind the pectoralis muscle may experience more discomfort than patients in whom the breast implant was placed directly under the breast tissue. Both are readily controlled with oral analgesics.

As with any surgical procedure, small sensory nerves to the skin are interrupted during surgery, and portions of the nipple/areolar complex may feel some degree of numbness. Sensitivity usually returns over several weeks, but some diminished feeling may last indefinitely. Patients may also experience a burning sensation and sensitivity to direct stimulation in their nipples for about two weeks. In general, patients should avoid sun exposure or use of a tanning bed until the numbness of the breasts has subsided. Thereafter, for at least six months, the incision should be protected with sunscreen of at least SPF 15.

Some swelling or bruising can be expected for approximately three to five weeks postoperative. This swelling will make the breast more firm and full. However, the breasts may not attain their final appearance or feel for three to four months (Figure 17–5).

Even after breast implant surgery, gravity and the effects of aging will eventually alter the size and shape of virtually every woman's breasts. Migration (shifting) of the implants can also occur several months postoperative.

Increasing pain, erythema, or drainage from the surgical wound should be reported to the surgeon immediately. This may represent

> Several large studies have demonstrated that women with gel or saline breast implants do not have an increased risk for connective tissue and autoimmune disease (e.g., scleroderma, lupus, fibromyalgia, and many others).

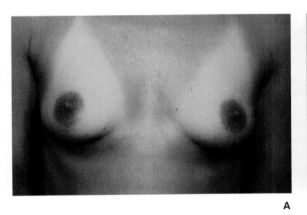 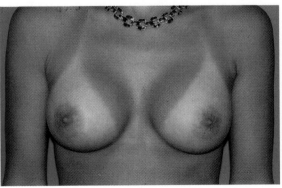

A   B

Figure 17–5

A, Preoperative patient. B, Postoperative patient. Photographs courtesy of David Rapaport, MD, plastic surgeon, Park Avenue, N.Y.

an infection. Although rare, if it occurs, it is most often seen within a week or two after surgery.

Although breast implants are well tolerated, the body considers them foreign, and the body's natural reaction to a foreign material is to surround it with a thin membrane called a "capsule." In some cases, this capsule can shrink around one or both implants, compressing the implant and making it round and hard. This is called **capsular contracture** and can occur in varying degrees. Severe capsular contractures can cause discomfort or changes in the breast's appearance (i.e., distortion). Capsular contracture may occur from a few weeks to several years after the initial procedure. If a patient does develop capsular contracture, surgical intervention may be required.

Patients who have nursed a baby within the year before augmentation may produce milk for a few days postoperatively.

Scars

All scars are permanent and their height, width, and final color are never completely predictable. Although scars will never disappear completely, they will be pink for several months and then gradually fade. The scars may remain the same size for several months or widen with time. However, the scars are usually unnoticeable to the casual observer.

POSTPROCEDURE ACTIVITIES

Patients are likely to feel tired and sore for a few days postoperatively, but they will be up and around in one to two days. Although patients may be able to return to work within a few days (depending on the level of activity required for their job), they should avoid much physical contact for two to three weeks after surgery.

To avoid unnecessary pressure on the recently operated breasts, most surgeons recommend that patients sleep on their back for several weeks postoperative. Patients are also encouraged to do deep breathing exercises to prevent atelectasis.

Patients must not lift anything for the first two weeks and *no heavy lifting* for the first three to four weeks. Vigorous activities, especially arm movement, may be restricted for two to three weeks.

SOME RISKS AND POSSIBLE COMPLICATIONS

The following are possible risks to breast implants:

If the implant is placed under the pectoral muscle, simple movement of the arms automatically moves the implant around in its pocket. Thus, some surgeons believe that putting the implants behind the pectoralis muscle may reduce the potential for capsular contracture. Statistically there is a slight difference in capsular contracture rates for silicone gel-filled implants placed subpectoral versus submammary.

If a saline-filled implant breaks, the implant will deflate in a few hours to days and the body will harmlessly absorb the saline solution, resulting in asymmetric breasts that will need to be repaired. On the other hand, if a break occurs in a **gel-filled breast implant,** it may not be so readily apparent because the silicone gel usually remains within the capsule that surrounded the implant. If, however a leak is diagnosed, it is recommended by the FDA to have it replaced. There has been some controversy regarding gel-filled implants that has all but been resolved over the past several years. However, the FDA recommends exchanging gel-filled implants every 10 years to minimize any risks of problems with silicone leakage.

> Rupture of **saline-filled breast implants** or silicone gel-filled breast implants can occur as a result of trauma to the chest or spontaneously, with no apparent cause.

- Bleeding/hematoma
- Infection
- Sensory changes in nipple/areolar complex(s)
- Capsular contracture
- Rupture of implant
- Migration (shifting) of the implants

Chapter 18

Breast-Lift Mastopexy

With age the breast skin loses its elasticity and factors such as pregnancy, nursing, and gravity often cause the breasts to sag. In addition, some women may also have stretch marks and loss of volume in their breasts due to weight fluctuations and natural breast atrophy. This droopiness of the breasts (ptosis) results because the skin envelope is much larger than the volume of breast tissue. This can be remedied through a breast-lift (mastopexy), a surgical procedure designed to make the breasts perkier, fuller, and more youthful looking.

INDICATIONS

If the patient's nipples are below the level of the inframammary crease when standing, they are candidates for a breast-lift. Although breasts of any size may be lifted, the best results are usually achieved in women with *small*, sagging breasts. Because of the greater weight, women with large breasts will most likely have shorter lasting effects (Figure 18–1).

Mastopexy does nothing in the way of increasing the breast volume. Thus, if a patient wants to be larger, breast implants can be inserted at the same time the breast-lift is performed.

The best candidates for mastopexy, as for all cosmetic procedures, are healthy, emotionally stable women with realistic expectations.

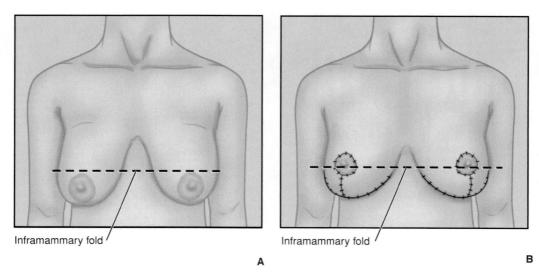

Inframammary fold

Inframammary fold

A

B

Figure 18–1

A, Ptosis of the breasts. B, After mastopexy.

Although breast-lift surgery will not increase the risk of developing breast cancer, depending on the patient's age or family history of breast cancer, a baseline mammogram may be recommended before surgery, and another mammographic examination some months after surgery. This will assist in mammogram interpretation of possible future changes in the breast tissue. *After a breast-lift, patients will still be able to perform self-examinations of the breasts.*

MECHANISM OF ACTION AND TARGET TISSUES

Because the main cause of droopy breasts is skin laxity and/or atrophy of the breasts, the goal of a breast-lift is essentially a tailoring of (reduction) the skin envelope such that it drapes over the available breast tissue to create a perkier and fuller breast—with a more natural placement of the nipple/areolar complex and overall contour.

Breast-lift procedures can be done through different incision patterns to place the resulting scar in such a manner as to camouflage it within creases or boundaries of sharp color demarcations (e.g., the dark areolar). They can include a circumareolar incision, a vertical incision (connecting the circumareolar incision to the inframammary incision), and a horizontal incision beneath the breast—much like the incisions for a breast reduction. In some instances, it may be possible to avoid the horizontal incision beneath the breast.

After the cosmetic surgeon removes excess breast *skin,* the nipple/areolar complex is shifted to a more youthful position on the resulting breast mound. The nipple/areolar complex remains attached to underlying mounds of breast tissue. This usually allows for the preservation of sensation and the ability to breast-feed.

PREPROCEDURE CONSIDERATIONS

The size and shape of the breasts, the size of the **areolas**, and the extent of sagging are factors to consider in selecting the best surgical approach to optimize the effect and reduce the appearance of the resulting scars. The surgeon will examine the breasts and measure them while the patient is in the sitting or standing position.

Although mastopexy usually does not interfere with breast-feeding, pregnancy is likely to stretch the breasts again and offset the results of a breast-lift procedure. Thus, patients planning to have more children should postpone a mastopexy.

Patients should make arrangements ahead of time for someone to drive them to and from their procedure and to assist them with their daily activities during the recovery period.

Anesthesia

A breast-lift surgery can be performed using local anesthesia and intravenous sedation to make the patient feel drowsy and relaxed, or with general anesthesia, causing the patient to sleep during the entire procedure.

PROCEDURE/TECHNIQUES

For cost containment and convenience, a breast-lift is usually performed on an outpatient basis, in the surgeon's office-based surgical suite, an outpatient surgery center, or hospital.

There are two types of breast-lift procedures: the full lift and the modified lift. Mastopexy usually takes one and a half to three and a half hours. The length of the procedure varies according to the surgeon's experience and technique used. If the patient is also having a breast implant inserted along with the breast-lift, it will be placed in a pocket directly under the breast tissue, or deeper, under the pectoralis muscle of the chest wall. Regardless of the technique, the nipple/areolar complex is repositioned to the approximate level of the inframammary crease—as viewed from an upright, lateral profile. Then, the incisions are closed with interrupted (buried) subcuticular sutures and running or interrupted (superficial) nonabsorbable sutures.

The Full Breast-Lift ("Anchor-Shaped" Incision)

This is the most common procedure for breast-lift; it involves an anchor-shaped incision following the natural contour of the breast.

Figure 18–2

The "anchor" incision.

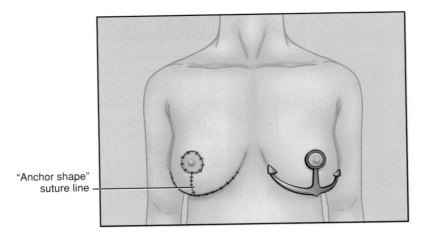

"Anchor shape" suture line

This method involves three incisions: one incision is made around the areola; this is followed by a second incision that runs horizontal to and parallel with the inframammary crease of the breast; and a third incision runs vertically from the six o'clock edge of the circumareolar incision to the inframammary incision (Figure 18–2).

The Modified Breast-Lift ("Doughnut Mastopexy")

Some patients with relatively small breasts and minimal sagging may be good candidates for this modified procedure, which only requires a circumareolar incision. This is also known as a "doughnut mastopexy" because a doughnut-shaped area of skin is excised around the dark area of the areola (Figure 18–3). If desired, areolas can be reduced in size for a more proportional appearance with the new breast.

With either technique, small drain tubes may be placed in the breasts to help avoid the accumulation of fluids. If the recovery period is uneventful, the patient may be permitted to go home after a few hours.

DRESSINGS AND WOUND CARE

Gauze or other dressings are usually placed on the breasts and covered with an elastic bandage, and/or the patient is placed in a surgical support bra. The latter should be worn around the clock for three to four days. It is then replaced with a soft support bra to be worn for three to four weeks postoperative.

Figure 18–3

Doughnut mastopexy incision.

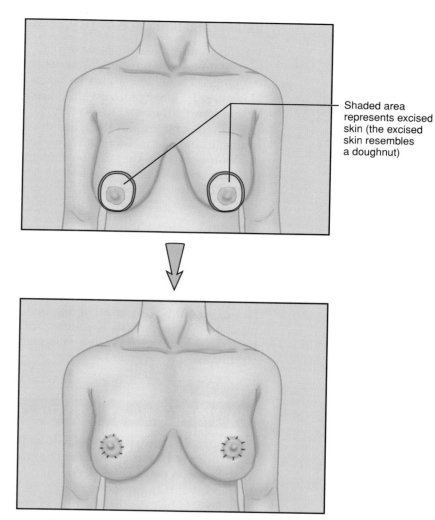

Shaded area represents excised skin (the excised skin resembles a doughnut)

The areola is then sutured to the surrounding skin

Once the anesthesia has worn off, it is normal for most patients to experience some discomfort. This is relieved by oral medication.

If the breast skin is very dry after surgery, patients can gently apply a moisturizer several times a day, and it is important to keep the moisturizer away from the suture lines.

Sutures

Generally, stitches will be removed in stages over a period of weeks. Most of the superficial sutures will be removed in 7 to 10 days. A few key stitches may be left in position a little longer.

Bathing and Hair Care

Washing hair can usually resume a couple of days after surgery; however, extreme care must be taken not to lift the arms until cleared by the surgeon. Care must also be taken not to get the dressing wet. However, if a waterproof dressing was used, the bra and gauze may be temporarily removed to shower.

Showers can resume once the drain is out, there is no further drainage, and the incisions are dry; sometimes patients can shower sooner if cleared by the surgeon. Patients should *not soak in tubs* until the incisions are completely healed. The incisions should be gently blotted dry, not scrubbed.

Makeup

Makeup can resume the day after surgery.

Sun Protection

Sun exposure or use of a tanning bed should be avoided until the numbness of the breasts has subsided. Afterward, the patient must protect the incision site with a sunscreen of at least SPF 15 for at least six months.

POSTPROCEDURE SKIN/TISSUE CHANGES

After surgery, there is an immediate and dramatic change in the shape of the breasts. However, they may be swollen and bruised for approximately one to two weeks, but the discomfort should not be severe. In addition, patients can expect some numbness in the nipple/areolar complex and breast skin. Over the ensuing six weeks, as the swelling subsides, this numbness usually fades. In some patients, however, it may last longer, and occasionally it may even be permanent. The breasts may require several weeks to assume a more natural shape. Incisions will initially be red or pink in color, remaining this way for many months after surgery.

Small nerves to the skin may be interrupted, causing the nipple/areolar complex to feel numb or have a less than full feeling. Sensation generally returns over several weeks, although some diminished feeling may last indefinitely. This does not usually interfere with erotic sensation.

The loss of elasticity that caused the original sagging of the breast can recur; there is no surgery that can permanently delay the effects of gravity, pregnancy, aging, and weight fluctuations.

Scars

Although incisions for mastopexy are strategically placed in locations that tend to be unnoticeable to the casual observer, these incisions often remain lumpy and red for months, then gradually fade to thin white scars. In most patients, the scars from the incisions will be pink for about six months and gradually fade thereafter. Fortunately, the incision(s) is/are placed so that patients can wear low-cut tops. Although certain individuals may have scars that are quite apparent, most scars from a breast-lift will heal and fade over time. However, the scars will always be visible upon close examination, because scars—no matter how well they heal—are permanent and their height, width, and final color are never completely predictable.

POSTPROCEDURE ACTIVITIES

Patients usually return home the same day and are usually instructed to sleep on their back or side to avoid pressure on their breasts. The day after surgery, most physicians instruct their patients to resume light activity. Any surgical drains will be removed within a few days of surgery, at which time the dressings may also be changed or removed. Patients may be instructed to wear a support bra for a few weeks, until the swelling and discoloration of their breasts diminish.

After several days, patients should be able to move about more comfortably. Straining, bending, and lifting must be avoided because these activities might contribute to swelling or even bleeding. Most women return to their usual activities, including work, in a week or so, depending on their job. In many instances, patients can resume most of their normal activities, including some form of mild exercise, after several weeks. They may continue to experience some mild, periodic discomfort during this time, but such feelings are normal.

Patients are usually instructed not to lift anything heavier than a gallon of milk for the first two weeks and no heavy lifting for three to four weeks; they should also avoid lifting anything over their head for three to four weeks.

Any sexual activity should be avoided for a minimum of one to two weeks, sometimes longer. After that, care must be taken to be extremely gentle with the breasts for the next several weeks.

SOME RISKS AND POSSIBLE COMPLICATIONS

No procedure is without risks; however, the majority of complications known to be associated with a breast-lift are minor when properly trained, certified, and experienced surgeons perform the procedure. Fortunately, significant complications from breast-lifts are infrequent. Every year, many thousands of women undergo successful breast-lift surgery, experience no major problems, and are pleased with the results. Some potential complications include:

- Bleeding
- Infection
- Reactions to anesthesia
- Asymmetry of breast mound and/or nipple/areolar complex
- Loss of sensation of breast mound and/or nipple/areolar complex
- Scarring

Chapter 19

Breast Reduction
Reduction Mammaplasty

Women with large, pendulous breasts often experience an assortment of troublesome symptoms, including, but not limited to, back and neck pain, skin irritation, physical deformities, and breathing problems. Breast reduction, technically known as *reduction mammaplasty,* is a surgical procedure to create smaller, better-shaped, proportional breasts. Breast reduction surgery has among the highest patient satisfaction rate of any cosmetic and reconstructive surgical procedure.

INDICATIONS

Women from their teens into their 80s can have breast reduction surgery. In general, it is usually wise to wait until at least age 20 to make sure the breasts have stopped growing.

Breast reduction surgery is usually not done for appearance alone; it is done to reduce the size of **pendulous breasts** for the purpose of relieving medical problems and symptoms caused by the weight of unusually large breasts. These symptoms include one or more of the following:

- Back and neck pain
- Bad posture and deformities of the skeleton
- Breathing problems
- Pain from sports or vigorous activity
- Chronic back, upper neck, and shoulder pain
- Skin rash under the breasts
- Deep, painful grooves in the shoulders from the pressure of bra straps

- Restricted levels of activity
- Self-esteem problems, particularly adolescent girls
- Difficulty wearing or fitting into certain bras and clothing

MECHANISM OF ACTION AND TARGET TISSUES

Breast reduction surgery is a tailoring/sculpting surgical procedure that reduces the size of large, pendulous breasts to make them less weighty. Unlike mastopexy, where only the skin is removed, breast reduction surgery also removes excess fibrous and fatty breast tissue. Because the size and weight of the breasts are the cause of the symptoms, reducing the size of the breasts results in reduction of weight and hence relief of the symptoms. Further, the overall appearance of the breasts may change after having a baby.

PREPROCEDURE CONSIDERATIONS

Women whose breasts are sagging but not too large might receive more benefit from a breast-lift, also known as mastopexy.

Before the surgical procedure, the surgeon will examine, measure, and photograph the breasts. The photographs can be used for reference during and after the procedure.

Breast reduction surgery may decrease the ability to breast-feed. Therefore, a woman wishing to do so should probably delay the procedure until she has had all her children.

Anesthesia

Although breast reduction surgery will not increase the risk of developing breast cancer (depending on the patient's age or family history of breast cancer), a baseline mammogram may be recommended before surgery, as well as another mammographic examination some months after surgery. This will assist with the interpretation of future mammograms to rule out surgically induced changes in the breast tissue.

Breast reduction is most often performed under general anesthesia, causing the patient to sleep during the procedure.

PROCEDURE/TECHNIQUES

Most breast reduction surgeries are performed as an outpatient, and patients are usually allowed to go home within hours of the operation. However, if an extremely large amount of breast tissue is to be removed, the surgeon may require the patient to stay overnight in the hospital for monitoring.

Patients should make arrangements ahead of time for someone to drive them to and from their procedure and to assist them with their daily activities during the recovery period.

There are several surgical techniques available for breast reduction surgery, but the most common one involves an *anchor-shaped incision* that goes around the areola, down from the areolar incision to an

Figure 19–1

One of several surgical incisions used for breast reduction and mastopexy.

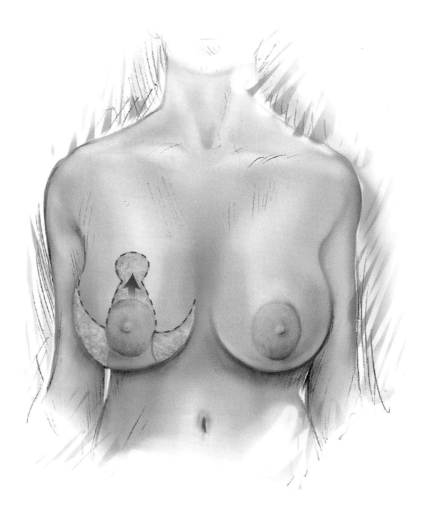

inframammary crease incision (Figure 19–1). Through this incision, the surgeon removes excess fat, breast tissue, and skin. This procedure can also reduce the size of the areola—the darker skin surrounding the nipple. The breast tissue is then redraped with the new skin envelope and sutured closed (Figure 19–2). Drainage tubes may also be placed to prevent accumulation of fluid for the first few days after surgery.

In most cases, the nipple/areolar complex remains attached to its blood supply and nerves. However, if the breasts are extremely large and droopy, the nipple/areolar complex may need to be removed and grafted to its new position. In such a case, the nipple/areolar complex permanently loses sensation and will also result in the patient's inability to breast-feed.

Figure 19–2

Resulting—sutured "anchor incision."

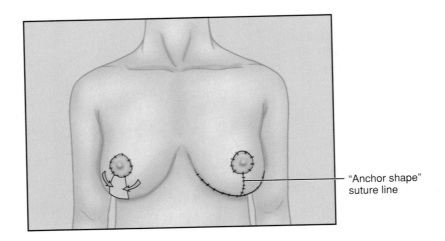

"Anchor shape" suture line

Bandages are applied to the breasts and the patient is fitted with a surgical bra for support. Depending on the size of the breasts and the surgical technique, breast reduction surgery generally takes about one to three hours per breast.

DRESSINGS AND WOUND CARE

The wounds are checked 24 to 48 hours after surgery. A small amount of fluid draining from the wound, and even some crusting around the incision, is normal. If present, drains are removed 1 to 2 days postoperative. The surgical bra is refitted and the patient is instructed to wear it continuously for 5 to 7 days. The surgeon may recommend a soft support bra to be worn for an additional 2 to 3 weeks.

There will be some pain and tenderness in the first day or two after the procedure that may last for a couple of weeks. However, most women require very little pain medication after the first 24 hours. The breasts may also be swollen, bruised, and sensitive for 3 to 4 weeks. The first menstruation after the operation may cause pain and swelling in the breasts. Recovery generally takes 5 to 6 weeks, although complete healing can take several months.

Sutures

Generally, sutures will be removed in stages over a period of weeks. Most of the superficial sutures will be removed in 7 to 10 days. A few key stitches may be left in a little longer.

Bathing and Hair Care

Women are advised not to shower for at least the first few days after surgery or until cleared to do so by their surgeon. Soaking in bathtubs is prohibited until the incision sites and all other wounds are completely epithelialized.

POSTPROCEDURE SKIN/TISSUE CHANGES

At first, the breasts may be somewhat bruised and swollen. This will gradually decrease. Small nerves to the skin are interrupted during surgery, and the area around the nipple/areolar complex and lower breast will have diminished sensation after the surgery. Sensitivity returns over several weeks, but some diminished feeling may last indefinitely. This does not usually interfere with erotic sensation. However, if the nipple/areolar complex required removal and grafting, the loss of feeling on the nipples will likely be permanent and the patient will no longer be able to breast-feed.

The breasts do not usually achieve their final shape immediately after surgery. It takes up to six months for everything to settle down. The vast majority of women maintain their results and do not require further surgery (Figure 19–3).

Scars

Incisions are strategically placed so that the resulting scar is usually unnoticeable to the casual observer. Initially, these scars are lumpy and red for more than six months, eventually fading to thin white lines. However, no matter how well they heal, the scars are permanent and their height, width, and final color are never completely predictable. They will always be visible upon close examination and certain individuals may have scars that are quite apparent. Patients are usually able to cover the resulting scars with a bra or swimsuit.

The results from breast reduction are so favorable that the patient's concern about pain and scarring is usually minimal.

POSTPROCEDURE ACTIVITIES

Although most women return to their usual activities in one week, the stress and strain of surgery leaves most women feeling fatigued for several weeks. However, women may be able to return to work in about two to three weeks if their job does not require strenuous activ-

Figure 19–3

Preoperative and postoperative pictures of breast reduction surgery. Reprinted with permission from *The American Journal of Cosmetic Surgery.*

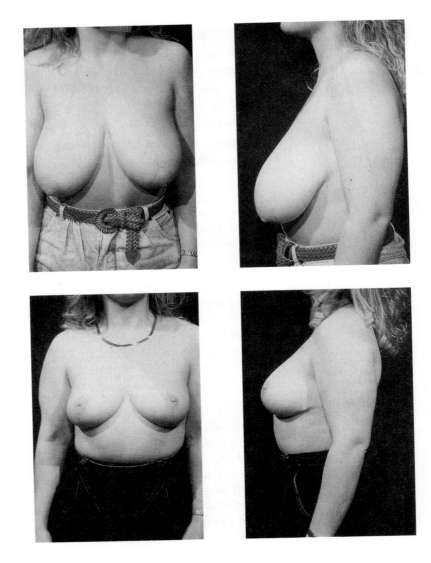

ity. If heavy lifting is required, it may take up to five or six weeks. Patients must not lift anything for the first two weeks and they should avoid raising their arms above their head for at least two weeks. Exercising should be limited to stretching, bending, and swimming for the first few weeks, until stamina returns. A good athletic bra is recommended for support.

SOME RISKS AND POSSIBLE COMPLICATIONS

No procedure is without risks; however, the majority of complications known to be associated with a breast reduction are minor when an experienced cosmetic surgeon performs the procedure. But as with any surgical procedure, there are risks and possible complications, including the following:

- Reaction to anesthetic
- Infection
- Bleeding
- Delayed wound healing
- Scarring
- Sensory loss in the nipples/areolar complex and/or breasts
- Impaired blood supply to the nipples, leading to loss of the nipples
- Inability to breast-feed
- Internal scarring that may make it difficult to read future mammograms
- Asymmetry in size, shape, position, and contour of the nipples/areolar complex
- Altered body image and possible risk of an adverse psychological reaction

Chapter 20

Tummy Tuck
Abdominoplasty

■ Leslie H. Stevens, MD, FACS

> A tummy tuck is not a weight-loss procedure or a substitute for exercise or a healthy diet.

Abdominoplasty, more commonly known as "tummy tuck," is a major surgical procedure that produces a smoother, firmer, flatter abdomen and a thinner waist. With some techniques, it even tightens the pubis and lifts the anterior thighs. An abdominoplasty can remove **striae distensae** ("stretch marks") between the umbilicus and the pubic area; those remaining are tightened, making them less noticeable.

INDICATIONS

The best candidates for *abdominoplasty* are men or women who are in relatively good shape but are bothered by redundant lower abdominal skin, excess fat, and/or weakened abdominal muscles that are unresponsive to diet or exercise. The surgery is particularly helpful to women who, through multiple pregnancies, have stretched their abdominal muscles and skin beyond the point where they can return to normal by dieting or exercising. Women who are planning a pregnancy should postpone an abdominoplasty accordingly. Abdominoplasty is becoming an even more popular operation with the increase in patients with massive weight loss after **bariatric surgery** (gastric bypass) for morbid obesity. If the abdominal wall musculature/**fascia** are firm and flat with minimal skin laxity, *simple liposuction* may be all that is required.

MECHANISM OF ACTION AND TARGET TISSUES

The tummy tuck is basically a tailoring procedure to recontour the abdomen and hips. The excess skin is excised and the remaining skin is repositioned over the umbilicus. If the abdominal wall (muscular layers) bulges out, it is tightened at the vertical midline.

PREPROCEDURE CONSIDERATIONS

Before the surgical procedure, the surgeon will perform a complete health history; because several factors contribute to the overall final result of a tummy tuck, a physical examination is performed to evaluate weight, skin elasticity, muscle tone, overall fat distribution, nutrition, and the extent of procedure needed. In general, patients who start out in top physical condition with strong abdominal muscles will recover from abdominoplasty much faster.

Smokers should quit smoking at least two weeks before surgery and not resume for at least two weeks after their surgery. Patients should avoid overexposure to the sun before surgery, especially to the abdomen, and they should avoid a radical diet, as both can inhibit the body's ability to heal.

Anesthesia

Either general anesthesia or regional/local anesthesia with intravenous sedation is used. The choice will depend on the extent of the procedure, the surgeon and anesthesiologist's preferences, and/or the patient's wishes. With the latter type of anesthesia, the patient will be awake, relaxed, and pain free; however, the patient may feel some tugging or occasional discomfort. With general anesthesia, the patient will sleep throughout the procedure.

PROCEDURE/TECHNIQUES

Many surgeons perform "tummy tucks" in an outpatient surgical center or an office-based facility; others prefer the hospital, where their patients have a brief stay. The patient's underlying health status will also play a role in deciding where the surgery is performed.

There are several different abdominoplasty techniques. The procedure of choice will depend on the extent of the laxity of the abdominal/

fascial wall, the redundancy of the skin, the elasticity of the skin, and the amount of fat. Several incisions can be used in this operation; they are placed in such a way that they are covered with most underwear and some bathing suit bottoms.

For a better body contour, liposuction of the surrounding area can be done in conjunction with the abdominoplasty.

Miniabdominoplasty

If the problem is localized between the pubic hairline and the umbilicus, a partial abdominoplasty can be performed. In this procedure, the incision is made just above the pubic hairline and extends laterally in the direction of the **anterior superior iliac spines**. If there is laxity in the muscle wall/fascia, this may be tightened with permanent, nonabsorbable sutures. The **cutaneous flap** (skin and underlying subcutaneous fat) is dissected from the underlying fascia of the abdominal muscle—from the pubic hairline up to the umbilicus.

After dissecting it from the underlying muscle/fascia, the cutaneous flap is stretched down to the incision line over the pubic hairline; the excess cutaneous flap is then excised and sutured into its new position. The length of the incision is determined by how much skin needs to be excised.

With partial abdominoplasty, the incision is much shorter and the umbilicus may not require surgical manipulation—unless, as the skin is tightened and stitched, the resulting tension pulls the umbilicus into an unnatural shape. If this occurs, a "buttonhole" is made in the centerline of the cutaneous flap to receive the umbilicus without distortion caused by the tension on the flap. Thus, it is possible to have a partial abdominoplasty without a scar around the umbilicus. Partial abdominoplasty may take an hour or two.

Full Abdominoplasty

The most common procedure is a full abdominoplasty. The incision is the same as in the partial abdominoplasty but may extend further laterally on to the hips. Moreover, the dissection of the cutaneous flap is more extensive; it is dissected from the underling muscular/fascia beyond the umbilicus and up to the ribs (Figure 20–1). Another incision is made around the umbilicus to free it from the cutaneous flap. If there is laxity of the abdominal muscle/fascia, it is tightened along the vertical midline with nonabsorbable sutures— from just above the pubic hairline up to the mid-portion of the rib

Figure 20–1

Extent of dissection (gray area) of the cutaneous flap.

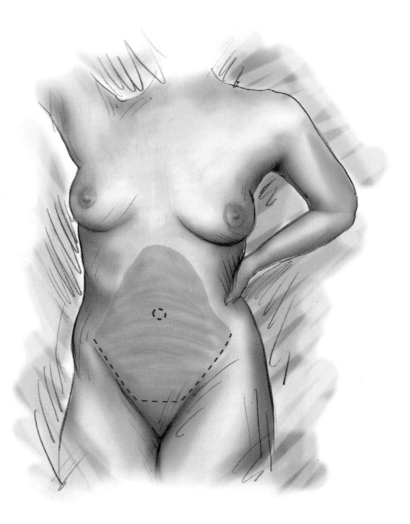

cage, creating a stronger, more contoured abdominal wall and a smaller waist (Figure 20–2).

Excess skin is then excised and a "buttonhole" opening is made to receive the umbilicus. The margin of the resulting large cutaneous flap is sutured to the skin margin, just above the pubic hairline (Figure 20–3). The umbilicus is then sutured into the "buttonhole" of the cutaneous flap. The incisions are usually closed in two to three layers—absorbable sutures in the deep fascia and dermis and absorbable or nonabsorbable sutures (or staples) for the closure of the skin.

Figure 20–2

The muscle/fascia tissue is tightened at the midline to help create a flat abdomen.

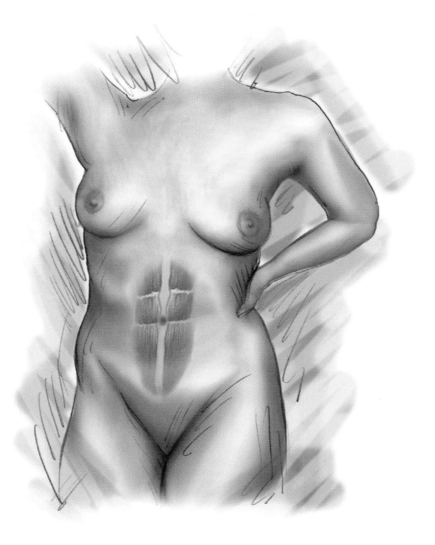

Temporary drains are usually inserted to prevent the buildup of excess serous fluid and/or blood within the surgical site. These drains can be either simple **penrose drains** that allow fluids to seep out from beneath the cutaneous flap to large absorbent pads, or **closed suction drains** that empty into a see-through collapsible bulb that can be drained by the patient.

Figure 20–3

Excess cutaneous tissue is pulled down, trimmed and sutured.

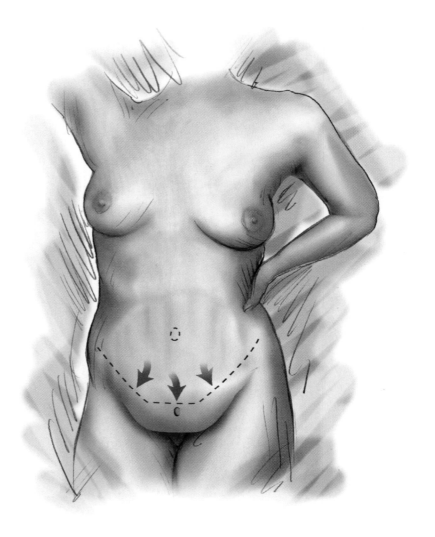

Steri-strips may be used over the suture line and covered with gauze, which is then covered with large absorbent pads. An abdominal binder or a pressure garment is then fitted over the dressing (Figure 20–4).

Complete abdominoplasty usually takes two to five hours, depending on the extent of work required and the surgeon's ability and experience. Depending on the extent of the surgery, the patient may be released within a few hours or may require a brief hospital stay.

Figure 20–4

Abdominal binder. Reprinted with permission from Shippert Medical.

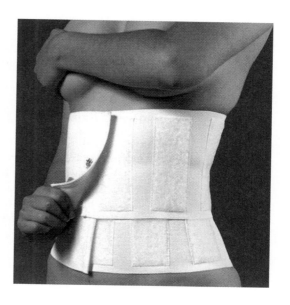

DRESSINGS AND WOUND CARE

Dressing may be kept in place by special tape and/or abdominal binder or support garment. The firm abdominal binders or pressure garments also serve to support the surgical area.

The dressings are usually checked in the surgeon's office the following day. These dressings will be changed according to the degree of drainage experienced. As the drainage decreases, the dressings and frequency of changes will change. Patients will usually be required to wear appropriate abdominal support for several weeks.

Drains

Drains serve to prevent the accumulation of fluid, which can interfere with the adhesion of the cutaneous flap to the underlying abdominal musculature/fascia. Patients are usually instructed on monitoring and emptying the drains for proper functioning. The drain(s) is/are usually removed within 5 to 7 days postoperative; their removal is usually painless. After the drain(s) is/are removed, the exit point(s) is/are covered with sterile absorbent gauze. The drain hole(s) will close by itself/themselves within 24 hours and the dressing(s) can then be removed.

Sutures

If external sutures or staples were used, they are usually removed within the first week postoperative. The deep absorbable sutures are left untouched.

Bathing and Hair Care

Washing hair can usually resume a couple of days after surgery; however, extreme care must be taken not to hyperextend the mid-abdomen. Care must also be taken not to get the dressing wet.

Showers can resume once the drain is out, there is no further drainage, and the incisions are dry, sometimes sooner if cleared by the surgeon. Patients should *not soak in tubs* until the incisions are completely healed. The incisions should be gently blotted dry, not scrubbed.

Makeup

Makeup can resume the day after surgery.

POSTPROCEDURE SKIN/TISSUE CHANGES

For the first few days postoperative, the abdomen will probably be swollen and the patient is likely to feel some discomfort, which can usually be controlled by oral *analgesics*. The surgeon may use a recent advancement in postoperative pain control, a nonnarcotic pain pump that dramatically reduces the amount of pain for the first three to five days. There may also be some bruising. Swelling may also occur and can take up to six weeks to resolve. Also, because the incisions interrupt the superficial network of nerves, there may be some numbness or diminished feeling sensation on the cutaneous flap and/or along the suture line. This returns to normal over several months but may last indefinitely in some areas.

Scars

With the exception of a partial abdominoplasty, patients can expect a circular scar immediately around the umbilicus and a low, horizontal curving scar just above the pubic hairline that can extend from hip to hip. As the scars heal, they may actually appear to worsen during the first three to six months. Scars will be red or pink for six months and will gradually fade.

All scars are permanent and their height, width, and final color are never completely predictable. It is not unusual for it to take up to a year or longer before scars flatten and lighten in color. Using silicone gel or sheeting on the incision has been shown to minimize the redness and thickening of the scar during the first few months of healing. In addition, bleaching creams may be prescribed for those patients who tend to heal with pigmented scars. The good news is that the scars usually will not show under most clothing, even under some bathing suit bottoms.

POSTPROCEDURE ACTIVITIES

Because each case and each patient is different, the surgeon will discuss resumption of activities with each patient on an individual basis.

Immediately postoperative, patients may not be able to stand straight; it is therefore necessary that they have someone take them home after the procedure and stay with them until they are able to care for themselves. Lying on one's back with the head elevated and knees flexed will relieve tension on the wound closure and should be practiced for the first week.

Patients are encouraged to walk to the bathroom (with assistance) as soon as possible. Exercise will help the patient heal better as well as reduce the likelihood of developing deep venous thrombosis. Walking may begin immediately postoperative to reduce swelling and lower the chance of blood clots, and light activities may begin within three days postoperative.

Depending on physical status, some patients may return to work after two weeks, whereas others may take four to six weeks to recuperate. Even patients who have never exercised before should begin an exercise program to reduce swelling, lower the chance of **blood clots**, and tone up muscles. The surgeon will determine the timing and extent of the exercises. Sit-ups should not be contemplated for several months after surgery! Vigorous exercise, especially weight lifting, should be delayed until there is a full recovery and/or it is cleared by the surgeon—usually in about six to eight weeks. It may take several weeks to feel completely back to normal.

SOME RISKS AND POSSIBLE COMPLICATIONS

The following are possible risks and complications to having a tummy tuck:

- Hematoma and/or **seroma** formation
- Infection
- Loss of skin

- Excessive scarring
- Localized sensory deficits
- Wound separation
- Necrosis of umbilicus
- Thrombophlebitis—blood clots in the deep veins of the legs (rare)
- **Pulmonary embolism**

Chapter 21

Liposuction
Suction-Assisted Lipoplasty

Liposuction is the most commonly performed cosmetic procedure in the United States. It is also known as **liposculpture**, **lipoplasty**, and **suction-assisted lipectomy (SAL)**.

INDICATIONS

Liposuction is a surgical procedure primarily used for the removal of stubborn areas of fat that will not respond to diet or exercise. Such areas can include the abdomen, hips, buttocks, thighs, knees, upper arms, cheeks, jowls, *submental* area (double chin), and breast tissue in men.

Whether to do a simple liposuction procedure and/or an accompanying "lift" procedure depends on the amount of excess skin versus the amount of excess fat. Although age is not a major consideration, older patients may have diminished skin elasticity and may not achieve the same results as a younger patient with tighter skin. **Cellulite**, or "dimpled" skin, will not be cured by liposuction.

Cellulite is a medical term used to describe an uneven, dimpled, "cottage cheese" texture to the skin overlying fat; it commonly appears on the buttocks, thighs, and/or hips. It is not responsive to liposuction because it is too superficial.

MECHANISM OF ACTION AND TARGET TISSUES

There are several liposuction techniques; they share a common principle of suction via a hand-held cannula that is inserted through a tiny stab wound incision (approximately 1.5 cm) in the skin. The cannula is connected to a suction machine via a flexible tube. For small areas, special cannulas are connected directly to a large hand-held syringe that generates suction. The hand-held cannulas have a blunt tip and holes along its shaft. Depending on the techniques, the fat is suctioned directly, or ultrasound waves break the walls of the fat cells, and the resulting fluid is suctioned through the cannula. The skin, muscles, nerves, and blood vessels are left intact.

There is an artistic component to the surgeon's ability to create the desired contour by manipulating the cannula to remove the appropriate amount of fat.

PREPROCEDURE CONSIDERATIONS

Avoid medications that affect blood coagulation.

Anesthesia

Local anesthesia, with a light sedative, spinal, or general anesthesia may be used in liposuction. Factors determining the type of anesthesia used include safety, effectiveness, the area and amount to be suctioned, the suction technique, and the level of comfort sought.

PROCEDURE/TECHNIQUES

Body contouring refers to the group of aesthetic procedures used to change the body contour. It includes abdominoplasty or tummy tuck, brachioplasty, liposuction, thigh buttock-lifts, reduction mammaplasty, and mastopexy (breast-lift).

Liposuction may be performed in an office-based surgical facility, in an outpatient surgery center, or in a hospital. In general, patients having *small* volume (<1.5 liter) liposuction usually return home the same day. For *large volume* (>1.5 liter) liposuction, an overnight stay for observation may be required to monitor blood pressure and fluid balance. Liposuction generally takes between one to four hours depending on the particular area, size of the area, type of anesthesia, and the technique used.

After a sterile preparation and draping with sterile barriers, a small "buttonhole" incision is made near the area where fat is to be removed; for example, for *submental* liposuction, the tiny stab incisions are placed behind the ear and one is placed just beneath the chin; for liposuction of the arms, a tiny incision is made near the elbow and/or in the armpit crease. The surgeon manipulates the cannula under the skin to contour the desired result (Figure 21–1).

In the early days of liposuction, *no fluid* was injected into the target area ("dry technique"). Today, *suction-assisted lipectomy* (SAL) is com-

Figure 21–1

Shaded areas represent suctioned areas.

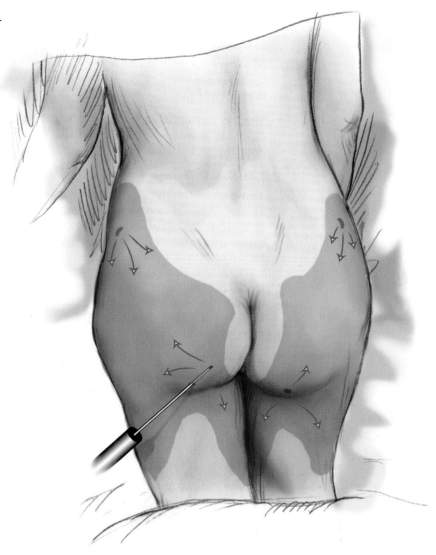

monly done using the *wet technique* with or without **ultrasound-assisted liposuction (UAL)**. The particular technique will be determined by a combination of factors, including the precise area to be treated, the amount of fat to be removed, and the surgeon's training, experience, and preference.

Dry Technique

The original technique (now mostly abandoned) did not involve the injection of fluids into the treatment area (e.g., only an *anesthetic* with *epinephrine* [vasoconstrictor] was injected).

Wet Technique

The wet technique is broken down into the *tumescent technique* and the *super-wet technique.* These two differ in the amount of fluid injected into the treated area.

Tumescent Technique

This technique involves injecting a large volume of solution into the area(s) to be treated before suctioning. Sometimes as much as three times the amount of fat to be removed is injected (3:1 ratio). The solution is a mixture of saline, lidocaine, and epinephrine (a vasoconstrictor). This fluid mixture causes the compartments of fat to become swollen and firm or "tumesced." This in turn reduces blood loss, reduces bruising, and provides anesthesia while facilitating the removal of fat. Although the **tumescent liposuction** can be used on any area of the body, it is commonly used on areas that require enhanced precision, such as the face, neck, arms, calves, and ankles.

Super-Wet Technique

This technique is similar to the tumescent technique, except that lesser amounts of fluid are used. Usually the amount of fluid injected is equal to the amount of fat to be removed (1:1 ratio).

Ultrasound-Assisted Lipoplasty (UAL)

UAL is done with a "wet technique" and requires the use of a special cannula that produces ultrasonic energy that breaks down the walls of the fat cells to liquefy the fat. The liquefied fat is then suctioned out. It is also commonly used in secondary procedures, when enhanced precision is needed. UAL is smoother and mechanically more efficient; it minimizes trauma, bruising, and blood loss. It is particularly useful on difficult-to-treat fibrous areas of the body, such as the enlarged male breast, the upper abdomen, and the upper back.

In general, UAL takes longer to perform than traditional liposuction.

DRESSINGS AND WOUND CARE

Patients will likely experience some fluid drainage from the small incisions. Thus, absorptive pads are applied to the incision sites, and the

Figure 21–2

Compression garment for
thighs, abdomen, and hips.
Reprinted with permission
from Annette International.

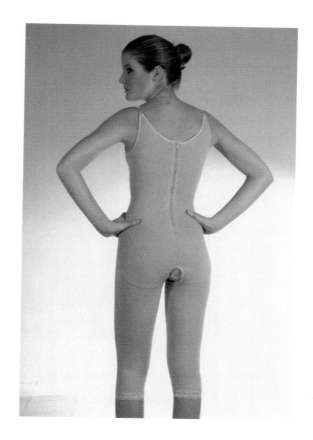

patient is fitted with a snug compression garment. The dressing is changed as needed or according to the surgeon's instructions. This garment is worn continuously for several weeks. The compression garment (Figures 21–2 and 21–3) helps keep the dressings in place and cuts down on postoperative swelling until the tissues have adjusted.

Sutures

Some surgeons choose to suture the tiny stab wounds that serve to introduce the cannula into the subcutaneous space; others allow them to heal on their own. If nonabsorbable sutures were used, they are usually removed in 7 to 10 days; if absorbable, subcutaneous sutures were used, they are allowed to dissolve on their own.

Figure 21–3

Compression garment for submental (double chin) area. Reprinted with permission from Shippert Medical and Design Veronique.

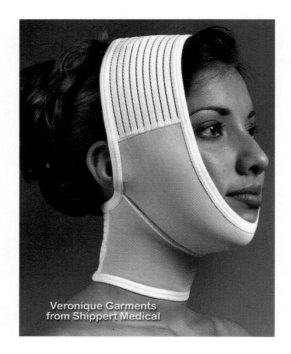

Bathing and Hair Care

Showers can resume as soon as the tiny stab wounds are healed or immediately, according to the surgeon's preference. Sometimes, patients can resume showering sooner if cleared by the surgeon. Soaking in a tub should only be done if the wounds are completely healed or cleared by the surgeon. If the head and neck area are not part of the surgical area, hair care can be resumed anytime after the surgery. If the surgical area is in the face area, hair care should not be done until cleared by the surgeon.

Makeup

If the head and neck area is not part of the surgical area, makeup can be applied anytime after the surgery. If the surgical area is in the face area, care should be taken not to get the makeup on or near the tiny stab wounds until cleared by the surgeon.

POSTPROCEDURE SKIN/TISSUE CHANGES

For the first day or two after surgery, most patients experience swelling in the treated areas. They will experience some degree of

Figure 21–4

Preliposuction and postliposuction of the thighs. Reprinted with permission from *The American Journal of Cosmetic Surgery.*

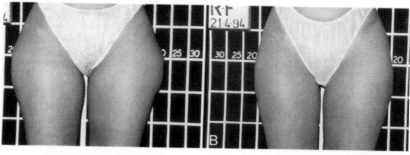

BEFORE LIPOSUCTION   AFTER LIPOSUCTION

pain, burning, bleeding, and temporary numbness in and around the treated area. Patients having arm liposuction may experience arm stiffness for a few days.

Patients will see a noticeable difference in the shape of their body soon after surgery. However, improvement will become even more apparent after four to six weeks. By this time most of the swelling has subsided. After about three months, any persistent mild swelling usually disappears and the final contour will be visible; however, some swelling may remain for six months or more (Figure 21–4).

Skin surface irregularities after large volume liposuction are not uncommon, particularly in older patients, who have lost their skin elasticity. This can include baggy skin, skin waviness, dimpling, and lumpiness. Fortunately, the incidence of these complications decreases significantly with the physician's experience.

Scars

The scars from liposuction are from the small stab wound incisions used to introduce and manipulate the cannula. These stab wounds are strategically placed to camouflage its location. They will be red or pink for six months and will gradually fade; most are barely visible. Although all scars are permanent, their final appearance can never be completely predictable. Internally, there is scarring that occurs in the dead space from where the fat cells have been removed. Initially there is *induration,* or firmness of the surrounding tissue, and eventually the scar softens such that it is imperceptible to touch.

POSTPROCEDURE ACTIVITIES

Most liposuction patients are usually mobile immediately after surgery. Sometimes an extra day or two of bed rest may be needed, particularly when large amounts of fat are removed. Mild activity in the initial postoperative period allows for better drainage and reabsorption of fluids, and it decreases stasis of blood flow in the extremities, which may help prevent blood clots in the legs.

Depending on the extent of the areas treated, most people return to work and resume their normal activities within days. Patients having *arm liposuction* may usually resume their normal activities within one week.

Mesotherapy, or *injection liposculpture,* is performed by microinjection of minute amounts of concentrated agents (conventional and/or homeopathic medications, plant extracts, vitamins, and nutrients) into the skin at various depths and amounts depending on the anatomic area or diagnosis. Mesotherapy may include diet, exercise modification, and oral supplements to achieve the desired result.

As with liposuction, healthy patients of stable weight who are troubled by small areas of lipodystrophy (fatty deposits) are candidates.

It is postulated that mesotherapy appears to accelerate lipolysis in the treated areas. Unlike liposuction, there is no general anesthesia, no need for surgery, and no bandages to wear. There is no downtime.

SOME RISKS AND POSSIBLE COMPLICATIONS

Though rare, complications can and do occur, regardless of applied technique. The risk of serious complications increases with the combination of several factors (e.g., removing large amounts of fat, having multiple procedures, and receiving general anesthesia). In addition, liposuction carries greater risk for individuals with medical problems such as diabetes, significant heart or lung disease, poor blood circulation, or those who have recently had surgery near the area to be contoured.

Modern low-power UAL units are basically free of burns to skin. However, with the exception of older *ultrasound-assisted lipoplasty* units, which may cause heat burns to the skin, all liposuction techniques share the same minor risks and complications:

- Minor wound healing problems
- Sensory deficit
- Infection
- Pigmentation changes
- Blistering of the skin from garment irritation
- Hematoma/seroma formation
- Asymmetry
- Baggy skin
- Skin waviness
- Dimpling
- Lumpiness

Section Four

Oral Antioxidants and Skin Care

Chapter 22

Oral Antioxidants and the Skin

■ R. H. Keller, MD, MS, FACP

With an average surface area of about 20 square feet, it is no wonder that the skin is subject to the greatest probability of premature aging. It is constantly being exposed to toxic substances and UV radiation that can produce **free radicals**, which have been implicated in UV sun damage, aging, and carcinogenesis of the skin.

It is naïve to claim that nutrition will wipe out skin wrinkles or stop skin aging. On the other hand, this has not been achieved by the multibillion-dollar cosmetic makeup industry. As will become clear in this chapter, with proper antioxidants and other nutrients, and proper sun protection, the aging clock, as apparent on the skin, can be retarded and, to a significant degree, reversed.

Most cosmetic formulations, although there are notable exceptions, do not penetrate into the dermis; they just sit on the skin until the next bath. Nonetheless, if used properly, many of these formulations serve a useful function (e.g., humectants, moisturizers, emollients, and, of course, sun block). Yet, when one considers that nutrition and supplements can be good for many systemic diseases, including fighting cancer, it is not farfetched to reason that ingested and properly absorbed nutrients stand a better chance of being delivered to—and metabolized by—the skin.

> **Skin Aging**
> Skin aging includes but is not limited to wrinkles, blotchiness, roughened texture, a sallowed coloration, and sagging. It is related to genetics, lifestyle, nutrition, a buildup of free radicals, UV radiation, and decreased gastric absorption of certain **antioxidants** and nutrients.

FREE RADICALS

To understand how antioxidants work, it is important to understand their target (i.e., *free radicals*). Free radicals are a natural biologic

Ironically, the atmospheric oxygen that is essential for keeping us alive is also the main culprit in human cancer and aging! Thus, breathing pure oxygen for prolonged (nonmedical) periods of time does not seem like a wise thing to do.

Some Known Toxins That Produce Free Radicals

- Ultraviolet irradiation, including UVA and UVB
- Aerosolized pollutants
- Smoking and second-hand smoke
- Excessive alcohol consumption
- Heavy metal exposure
- Exposure to some clothing fabrics—with or without additives
- Radiation
- Exercise
- Inflammation
- Certain drugs

Absorption of antioxidants and nutrients is limited by the secretion of hydrochloric acid (HCl) in the stomach, which diminishes with age. To circumvent this problem, one might consider taking betaine, which acts like hydrochloric acid to ensure the adequate breakdown of protein into the constituent amino acids as well as a daily (absent lactose intolerance) whey shake, which maximizes absorption of amino acids.

process that results from the body's use of oxygen and even UV radiation. Free radicals damage DNA, cytoskeletal elements, cellular protein, and cellular membranes.

With an even number of electrons, oxygen is a stable molecule. However, when it combines with other molecules in the body, the electrons are no longer even, and the oxygen molecules become unstable and are termed "free radicals." This is not to say that oxygen is the only molecule capable of becoming a free radical. Interestingly, even an antioxidant, once used, becomes a *free radical* itself. It is analogous to playing *"you're it."*

A large, and growing, number of experimental and, more importantly, clinical studies demonstrate unequivocally that certain nutrients and antioxidants can affect *free radicals* to not only slow or prevent age-related DNA damage but also to enhance the body's ability to repair the damage after it occurs.

Not surprisingly, this growing knowledge has increased public awareness of antioxidants as protective ingredients for the prevention of UV-mediated skin damage, as well as for the prevention of wrinkles. Consequently, many antioxidants are now being incorporated in dietary supplements (**nutriceuticals**) and topical cosmeceuticals.

Cosmeceuticals comprise topical products containing scientifically proven ingredients designed to reduce and protect against signs of skin aging; in comparison, cosmetics merely cover up signs of aging. Unfortunately, the great majority of the former, even though they may have scientific sounding names, do not penetrate into the skin and simply wash off with the next shower. Adding collagen to skin creams is like laying boxes of nails on the roof in the hope of adding structural support to the house.

ANTIOXIDANTS

As one ages there is a buildup and cumulative effect of free radicals in the skin. Fortunately, the body has developed natural defense mechanisms, which protect against free radicals (i.e., antioxidants). The most prevalent antioxidant in the human body is **glutathione**.

Some antioxidants work with other antioxidants and nutrients in an interdependent ("networking") synergy to enhance their effect on limiting free radicals in tissues. These are known as "network antioxidants."

A number of independent and interdependent antioxidants are required to prevent ultimate tissue deterioration. To mitigate, if not prevent, the untoward effects of premature aging on the skin and the development of many of the degenerative diseases associated with aging, the antioxidants must be administered together with their "networking" partners.

Antioxidants Have Been Shown (Experimentally and/or Clinically) to:

Enhance the skin's:
- immune system
- moisture retaining capabilities
- ability to fight certain forms of skin cancer

Assist in:
- producing healthy keratinocytes
- sloughing off of damaged epidermal cells
- the prevention of facial wrinkles
- repairing skin damage caused by UV light

Increase:
- skin hydration
- the skin's epidermal thickness

Maintain:
- healthy subcutaneous fat for plump skin
- the elasticity of the skin

Decrease:
- the breakdown of collagen and promote healthier collagen
- facial pigmentation
- protect the skin barrier by decreasing the permeability of the skin

The *free radical* theory of aging explains why antioxidants are thought to prevent wrinkles, but this theory does not justify the use of antioxidants to treat wrinkles that are already present.

Alpha lipoic acid (ALA) represents a prototypic example of the interdependence of antioxidants as it regenerates the antioxidant activity of vitamin C and glutathione and, to an extent, vitamin E. In reciprocation, ALA's antioxidant activity is regenerated by both vitamins E and C, which also regenerates the antioxidant activity of glutathione.

ORAL ANTIAGING AGENTS AND THEIR EFFECT ON SKIN

Although arbitrary, we shall divide the skin's antiaging agents into six separate groups. These include vitamins, low molecular weight antioxidants, hormones, herbs, miscellaneous nutrients, and trace elements. Each of these function both as independent and interdependent ("networking") series and although they must, by logical necessity, be examined separately, we will attempt wherever possible to elucidate the interdependencies—although our knowledge in this area remains imprecise and further work in this subject is progressing.

Vitamins

Vitamin A

Vitamin A markedly reduces the effects of a major detrimental UV-induced skin free radical called lipid peroxide. This is of particular importance as lipid peroxides break down the subcutaneous fat, which together with collagen and elastin in the skin provide the plumpness of youthful skin.

Vitamin A is critical in producing epidermal cells (keratinocytes) as well as loosening the intracellular connection of epidermal cells, allowing damaged cells to slough off more readily and promote youthful, smooth, and a uniform pigmented appearance of the skin.

Although vitamin A is readily available over the counter, it is extremely important not to exceed the recommended daily allowance because it can accumulate in the body and result in liver and brain damage.

It has been well documented that sufficient vitamin A reduces the incidence of skin papillomas.

Beta Carotene

The body converts beta carotene into vitamin A as needed, and the excess beta carotene is available as an additional antioxidant, thus preventing the toxic buildup of *vitamin A.*

Vitamin C (Ascorbic Acid)

- Vitamin C works with glutathione to prevent the growth of new blood vessels. This is important because cancerous tumor growth requires new blood vessels.

By our forties or fifties we have already experienced a significant decline, if not the disappearance, of two major skin-protecting hormones: *melatonin* and *dehydroepiandrosterone (DHEA)*.

- Together with certain amino acids, it promotes the development of new collagen to help prevent wrinkles.
- Vitamin C significantly reduces the development of oncogenes, which are involved in photocarcinogenesis (tumor) production associated with UVA irradiation.
- Absorption of vitamin C decreases with age and is markedly reduced throughout the body by smoking as well as second-hand smoke.

Vitamin E

- When taken orally (or topically), vitamin E offers some photoprotection from UV irradiation, which is associated with sunburn, variegated pigmentation, **hyperplasia**, immunosuppression, and DNA damage.
- It protects cells from oxidative stresses that inhibit biosynthesis of collagen and elastin and provides protection against the attendant risk of skin cancer.
- There are several oral forms of vitamin E; a-Tocopherol (D form) has the best absorption, although others such as gamma tocopherol and tocotuenes also serve important functions.
- The potency of vitamin E as an antioxidant is enhanced by combination with other oral antioxidants, including Co Q-10 enzyme, and the combination has been shown to reduce the premature death of fibroblasts, which provide the scaffolding for the collagen, elastin, and subcutaneous fat that maintains the skin's youthful, plump appearance.
- Vitamin E has been shown to decrease the major inflammatory substances that break down the protective barrier of the skin.
- Vitamin E has a known blood thinning effect; therefore, some physicians may instruct patients to suspend vitamin E supplementation several weeks before surgery.

Low Molecular Weight Antioxidants

Although the vitamins already discussed represent major protection against the damage and aging of the skin, perhaps a more important protection resides in this group of elements collectively termed *low molecular weight antioxidants*. These antioxidants not only function as protective agents but, to a large extent, also recharge or recycle other skin protective antioxidants. Among these substances, perhaps the most prominent in antioxidant protection is glutathione.

Glutathione

- The most prevalent antioxidant in the human body
- Made up of three amino acids: *glutamate, cysteine,* and *glycine*

- Prevents the premature death of *keratinocytes* (skin cells) induced by UVB irradiation
- Functions predominantly in the mitochondria and, together with Co Q-10 enzyme and *carnitine,* maximizes the energy production (ATP) and health of all cells in the human body
- Protects the integrity of *collagen* and, to a lesser extent, *elastin*—two proteins most prominently involved in the elasticity and pliability of youthful skin. This protection is augmented by *carnosine* and *curcumin,* an extract of curry. Collectively they prevent the cross-linking of proteins to sugars (**glycation**), which inhibit further collagen synthesis and create skin rigidity
- In concert with *vitamin C, glutathione* protects the skin from UV-induced skin cancers
- Works both independently and interdependently with other small molecular weight antioxidants, including alpha lipoic acid
- Protects the skin from the damage associated with heavy metal and pesticide exposure
- Is also involved in regulating the melatonin production in the pigment-producing cells of the skin
- Its levels in the body are increased by vitamin A, vitamin C, and alpha lipoic acid
- Smoking as well as UV radiation decreases glutathione levels throughout the body

Alpha Lipoic Acid (ALA)

- This multifunctional skin antioxidant is both water and lipid soluble, allowing it to perform in all three layers of the skin and in all components, including the cell membrane, cytoplasm, nucleus, and all the associated organelles of the cells, including the mitochondria.
- It is involved in the breakdown of "glycated" collagen, which is a hallmark of aged and rigid skin.
- It retards, if not prevents, the production of inflammatory molecules, termed cytokines, which exacerbate the photo damage and skin aging induced by the sun, the environment, smoking, and other unhealthy factors.

Coenzyme Q-10

Coenzyme Q-10 is known to suppress the breakdown of collagen, the chief supporting matrix of the dermis. The level of *Co Q-10* declines with age. It is a useful antiaging treatment for the skin.

Hormones

DHEA and melatonin are important in maintaining the youthful appearance of the skin and, at the very least, retarding many of the degenerative diseases of aging.

Dehydroepiandrosterone (DHEA)

- In addition to protecting the vascular integrity of the skin, together with omega-3 fatty acids, it is a critical element in activating the body's immune defenses.
- In addition, along with other antioxidants, it has been shown to retard the development of a variety of cancers, including those that occur in the skin.
- DHEA stimulates the sebaceous glands, which act as part of the skin barrier and maintain the youthful (hydration) moisture-retaining properties of the skin.
- Together with vitamin A, they produce both the stimulation of keratinocyte production, the orderly maturation of keratinocytes, and the sloughing off of damaged keratinocytes, all of which foster and maintain youthful, healthy skin.
- DHEA increases collagen production and decreases collagen breakdown.
- Levels of DHEA peak at about 30 years of age. It then decreases with age. Therefore, DHEA is not recommended for people under 35.
- DHEA declines approximately 10 percent per decade.

It is important to be aware that DHEA can be converted into other hormones, and thus it is contraindicated in patients with elevated prostate specific **antigen** (PSA) levels, as well as men with prostate cancer and women with breast cancer. Therefore, one should consult a physician before taking DHEA supplements.

Melatonin

- This hormone is produced by the *pineal gland* in the brain and plays a major role in the maintenance of the skin.
- Unfortunately due to stress from any cause, the production of melatonin decreases with age and completely stops by age 35, resulting in a variety of changes, which cumulatively result in accelerated skin aging.
- Melatonin, in a manner similar to glutathione, protects the skin against oxidative damage from the sun and other environmental pollutants by scavenging free radicals. It also reduces the erythema, cellular, and DNA damage associated with UVA or UVB irradiation.
- It promotes the growth of new keratinocytes, which are crucial to the maintenance of youthful appearing skin.

Melatonin has been reported to promote delta, or deep wave sleep, and it is during this period of sleep that *"growth hormone,"* another critical skin antiaging hormone, is produced.

Herbs

There are a number of herbs that, in experimental studies, have demonstrated skin protective properties. These include quercitin, perhaps (although not completely proven) by regenerating *glutathione,* especially when skin is subjected to UVA irradiation. In a similar vein, *pycnogenol* and green tea extracts, particular those containing *genestin* and *silymarin* (better known by its alternate name, milk thistle), and *reservatol,* found in red wine, all demonstrate some protection against UV and environmental pollutant-induced skin damage in the skin.

Miscellaneous Nutrients

Amino Acids

The amino acids *proline, histadine, argenine,* and *ornithine,* as well as glutathione, are required for collagen synthesis. Amino acids (glutamate, cysteine, and glycine) are required for the body to synthesize *glutathione,* the most prevalent antioxidant in the human body.

Curcumin

Curcumin functions to prevent cross-linking between sugars and proteins *(glycation),* which prevents or at least inhibits new collagen synthesis, as well as creating rigid skin.

Carnosine

Carnosine not only prevents *glycation* but, to an extent, can reverse it and thus reestablish the production of new collagen as well as prevent/treat the age spots (liver spots) associated with aged skin.

Omega Acids

Omega acids offer significant benefit in reducing the incidences of many degenerative diseases of aging. These acids have also been demonstrated to reduce the erythema associated with UV irradiation by reducing inflammatory agents. They require vitamin E to prevent epidermal lipid peroxidation as well as participate in the maintenance of the subcutaneous layer of skin, which provides the plumpness associated with youthful skin.

It is of paramount importance, however, that omega acids be used at a dosage of 1,000 mg/day only with other antioxidants, including vitamin E, and, to a degree, vitamin K, as well as glutathione and melatonin, as omega-3 fatty acids alone can actually increase the sun damage to the skin.

Essential Trace Elements

Selenium

Selenium has known anti-inflammatory properties and offers UV protection. In addition, it offers immune protection and has an anticancer effect. *Selenium* is important for elasticity of tissue. It is also required to regenerate *glutathione*.

Copper

Copper is present in virtually every cell; it is the third most abundant element in the human body. It is important in the intracellular formation of copper-dependant enzymes, including superoxide dismutase, an antioxidant; in addition, it is essential for lysyl oxidase, which is involved in the cross-linking of elastin and collagen.

Magnesium

Magnesium is critical to the effective function of the bodily defenses (the immune system), which in effect raises the level of damage induced by reducing the synthesis of prostaglandin E2, which activates inflammatory cytokines that exacerbated UV-induced skin damage.

CONCLUSION

It is well known in the medical community that deficiencies of certain nutrients are known to cause various forms of skin conditions. A classic and historic example is the major lack of vitamin C, which is known to cause **scurvy**—a disease from insufficient vitamin C that leads to the formation of spots on the skin, spongy gums, and bleeding from almost all mucous membranes.

It is therefore not hard to understand how even mild deficiencies of vitamin C, which are common and often undiagnosed, would impair the skin's health to some degree. Although scurvy is a serious skin disease, it can be treated with high doses of oral vitamin C.

With the exception of nitroglycerine cream, which can penetrate the dermis to affect the vascular system, most heart medications need to be taken by mouth. So why not treat skin with oral agents that are scientifically and clinically proven to affect the skin?

The nutrients and antioxidants enumerated and explained in this chapter should serve only as a harbinger of further discoveries in aging. Although these antioxidants and nutrients should not individually, or collectively, be considered a panacea for antiaging, they certainly represent a definite beginning in retarding the ravages that cause premature aging of the skin. As this research continues to expand and be validated by corroborative studies, the list of these nutrients and antioxidants cannot but continue to grow.

Finally, in selecting which brand to choose, buyer beware. The public needs to be educated (e.g., not all vitamin E is equal, DHEA must be in the micronized form for optimal effect, and herbs should be checked for standardization of extracts to ensure that

A major deficiency in vitamin C leads to a disease called *scurvy*, which was particularly prevalent in seafarers in the eighteenth century—until it was determined that fresh limes, high in vitamin C content, could reverse scurvy. Thus sailors, especially from Britain, were known as *limeys*.

there is no contamination with pesticides, heavy metals, or other pollutants). For more information on vitamins and antioxidants visit www.vitimmune.com.

SUGGESTED READING

Bell, E., et al. (1991). Recipes for reconstituting skin. *J. Biomech Eng., 113*(2), 113–119.

Hu, H. L., et al. (2000, December 20). Antioxidants may contribute in the fight against aging; an in vitro model. *Mech Ageing Dev., 121*(1–3), 217–230.

Irshad, M., et al. (2002). Oxidant-antioxidant system: role and significance in human body. *Indian J Exp Biol., 40*(11), 1233–1239.

MacKay, D., et al. (2003, November). Nutritional support for wound healing. *Altern Med Rev., 8*(4), 359–377.

Rhie, G., et al. (2001, November). Aging and photoaging-dependent changes of enzymic and nonenzymic antioxidants in the epidermis and dermis of human skin in vivo. *Invest Dermatol., 117*(5), 121–127.

Varani, J., et al. (1998). Molecular mechanisms of intrinsic skin aging and retinoid–induced repair and reversal. *J. Investig Dermatol Symp Proc., 3*(1), 57–60.

Yu, B. P. (1999, November). Approaches to anti-aging intervention: the promise and the uncertainties. *Mech Ageing Dev., 111*(2–3), 73–87.

Zimmerman, J. A., et al. (2003, January–February). Nutritional control of aging. *Exp Gerontol., 38*(1–2), 47–52.

Section Five

Common Terms Used by Plastic Surgeons and Dermatologists

Glossary, 207

Glossary

A

abdominal binder   a broad, elastic, girdle-type bandage used to encircle the abdomen after abdominal liposuction or abdominoplasty.

abdominoplasty   the surgical removal of loose abdominal skin and fat to produce a smoother, firmer, flatter abdomen and a thinner waist. If *diastasis recti* is present, it may also be repaired.

ablation   the surgical excision of tissue. In *aesthetic medicine,* it is commonly used to describe vaporization of tissue with certain lasers.

ablative lasers   lasers that can vaporize tissue (e.g., as in skin resurfacing).

abrasion   a removal or loss of skin by scraping friction.

abscess   a collection of pus anywhere inside the body. These abscesses must be drained because antibiotics will not reach the bacteria within the abscess to be effective.

Accutane   a vitamin A-related compound that inhibits sebaceous gland function. It is used in the treatment of severe acne that is unresponsive to antibiotics.

actinic keratosis   flat, reddish, single, or multiple skin lesions, which commonly have a gritty, sandpaper-like feel on the surface. Although not a cancer, they have a serious potential to become cancerous if left untreated for a number of years.

active medium a LASER's energy source (solid, gas, or liquid) whose atoms are forced to produce photons.

adipose tissue fat tissue.

ad lib Latin abbreviation (ad libitum) meaning "to the full extent of one's wishes." Sometimes seen on doctor's orders (e.g., drink water as desired, or drink water ad lib).

advancement flap stretching cutaneous or myocutaneous tissue to cover an adjacent defect.

aesthetic of or relating to beauty.

aesthetician see *esthetician*.

aesthetic medical practitioner a medical doctor who performs certain elective procedures or surgery on patients to improve their physical appearance.

aesthetic medicine medical arts applied to enhance a person's physical appearance.

aesthetic surgery see *cosmetic surgery*.

age spot small, flat, pigmented spots most often seen on areas of the body with a history of excessive sun exposure over many years (e.g., dorsum of hands).

AHA see *alpha hydroxy acid*.

ala nostril.

alar rim the border of the nostril.

alar wedge excision excising a small segment of the lateral nostrils to narrow the nostrils.

alopecia complete or partial hair loss.

alpha hydroxy acid commonly used in (light) face peels.

ambulatory a term used in the medical field to identify someone who is able to walk about; also refers to outpatient procedures or surgery.

amino acids the building blocks of protein.

analgesics pain medications.

anaphylaxis an allergic response to an agent characterized by difficulty breathing; can be life threatening.

anchor-shaped incision a common incision used in *breast reduction* or *breast-lift* surgery.

anterior anatomic description, meaning in front of.

anterior superior iliac spines the most prominent point of the hip bones at the lower abdomen.

antibiotic   a pharmaceutical agent effective against bacteria.

anticoagulant   any agent that prevents normal blood clot formation, such as aspirin, warfarin, NSAIDs, and so on.

antifungal   any pharmaceutical agent effective against fungi or yeast.

antigen   a substance capable of stimulating an immune response.

antihistamine   a pharmaceutical agent that reduces the effect of allergic symptoms (e.g., Benadryl).

antioxidants   a substance that opposes oxidation or inhibits reactions promoted by "free radicals."

antiseptic cleanser   a topical substance that prevents or slows the growth of infection-causing organisms.

areola   the circular area of darker pigmentation surrounding the breast nipple.

atopic dermatitis   inflammation or irritation of the skin caused by an allergen.

atrophy   wasting of tissues.

augmentation mammaplasty   see *breast implants*.

autoimmune   production of antibodies against one's own cells or tissues.

autologen   a material derived from the patient's own skin that may be used to augment his or her lips.

autologous tissue   the use of the patient's own tissues in reconstructive or cosmetic surgery.

axillary   of or referring to the armpit.

azelaic acid   a bleaching agent to lighten the skin.

B

bariatric surgery   gastric reduction surgery for morbid obesity.

basal cell carcinoma   the most common type of skin cancer; occurs most frequently on the face; rare occurrence of metastasis.

BDD   see *body dysmorphic disorder*.

benign tumor   a noncancerous tumor.

betadine   an antiseptic solution frequently used to prepare the skin for surgery.

beta hydroxy acid   an agent used in face peels; also know as *salicylic acid*.

biopsy   excising tissue from living patients for a histologic (cellular) diagnostic examination.

blackhead   seen when a hair follicle is filled with a plug of oil, bacteria, and cells. The opening remains patent to the surface, and oxidation causes the surface of the plug to turn black.

bleaching agent   a pharmaceutical agent that slows or blocks the production of pigment- producing cells, used to lighten pigmented areas of the skin.

blepharitis   inflammation of the eyelids.

blepharochalasis   redundant skin in the upper eyelids.

blepharoplasty   surgery of the upper and or lower eyelids.

blepharoptosis   droopy eyelids.

blepharospasm   spasmodic winking of the eye; sometimes managed with Botox injections.

blister   skin bleb filled with clear fluid.

blood clots   abnormal coagulation of blood within the circulatory system or a hematoma.

blood thinners   medications that interfere with the normal clotting mechanism; helps prevent blood clots.

blue peel   a chemical peel using TCA with a blue-dye marker that helps determine the depth of the peel.

body contouring   to reshape a part of the body using liposuction, lipoinjection, or excision of excess tissue, as in *abdominoplasty* or *brachioplasty.*

body dysmorphic disorder   a psychiatric condition in which those afflicted are preoccupied with an imagined defect in their appearance.

Botox injections   a toxin that, when injected into specific muscles, temporarily blocks (paralysis) the nerve impulse to the muscle.

botulinum toxin   a toxin derived from *Clostridium botulinum* used in *aesthetic medicine* to treat dynamic wrinkles.

bovine   of or pertaining to a cow.

brachioplasty   excision of redundant skin and fat from the upper arms to improve contours.

BRAVA   a nonsurgical, external suction device used over a period of months to enhance breast size.

breast augmentation   see *breast implants.*

breast implants   to increase the size of the breast(s) using synthetic material (e.g., silicone, or saline in a silicone envelope).

breast-lift   a tailoring of (reduction) the skin envelope such that it drapes over the available breast tissue to create a perkier and fuller breast, with a more natural placement of the nipple/areolar complex and overall contour.

breast reduction   a tailoring/sculpting surgical procedure that reduces the size of large, pendulous breasts. Unlike *mastopexy,* where only the skin is removed, breast reduction surgery also removes excess fibrous and fatty breast tissue.

brow-lift   forehead-lift to elevate the brow and/or tighten the forehead skin.

BTX   Botox.

buccal fat pad   the fat pad just inferior to the cheek.

buttock-lift   excision of excess fat and loose skin in the buttock area.

C

cadaver   of or pertaining to a dead human body.

cafe-au-lait spot   a benign, flat, light brown to tan lesion.

calf implant   the subcutaneous silicone implant to increase fullness of the calf.

camouflage makeup   a flesh-toned cosmetic product used to cover scars, bruises, and skin discolorations.

cannula   a small, hollow tube used in liposuction.

canthus   the inner corner of the eye.

capillary   a tiny blood vessel that connects the arterial system to the venous system.

capsular contracture   a naturally forming scar tissue around a breast implant, which shrinks and tightens more than it should, making the breast feel firmer than normal and sometimes causing pain and distortion of the breast.

capsulectomy   surgical removal of the capsule scar tissue surrounding the breast implant.

carbolic acid   see *phenol.*

carcinoma   the medical term for cancer.

cartilage grafts   using a patient's own cartilage to rebuild or repair another part of his or her body.

cellulite a medical term that describes dimpled skin that is uneven ("cottage cheese" texture) due to a certain type of underlying fat; commonly appears on the buttocks, thighs, and hips.

cellulitis bacterial infection of skin and soft tissue causing redness and warmth due to local inflammatory changes; requires immediate medical attention.

cheek-lift surgery to raise the middle of the face to enhance cheek and under-eye fullness and contour; also called mid-face-lift.

chemical exfoliation chemical peel.

chemical peels applying chemicals on the surface of the skin to improve its appearance.

chloasma see *melasma*.

circumareolar of or related to the area around the areola.

closed rhinoplasty surgery of the nose involving internal incisions, which do not leave a visible scar.

closed suction drains drain tubes connected to a compressible bulb to collect fluid/blood from some surgical wounds in a closed system.

Clostridium botulinum a bacteria responsible for a life-threatening form of food poisoning.

clotting studies common preoperative lab studies to evaluate the clotting mechanism (e.g., PT, PTT, platelets, and bleeding time).

coagulation of or pertaining to the clotting of blood.

cold compress a cold pad or gauze used to retard swelling, bruising, and/or to soothe.

cold sores fever blisters caused by the herpes I virus.

collagen the major component of the extra-cellular matrix of a variety of connective tissues. In the skin, collagen is the major support matrix and accounts for approximately 80 percent of the total dry weight of the dermis.

columella the column at the base of the nose that separates the nostrils.

comedones enlarged hair follicles filled with sebum, dead cells, and bacteria. If they are open to the skin surface, they are known as blackheads or "open comedones." If they are closed to the skin surface, they are known as whiteheads or "closed comedones."

complication a secondary disease or condition that develops in the course of a primary disease or condition and arises either as a result of it or from independent causes.

computer imaging   using a computer program to simulate how one will look after a surgical or nonsurgical procedure.

congenital nevus   a pigmented skin lesion present at birth.

conjunctiva   a delicate mucous membrane that lines the inside of the eyelids and continues on to cover the sclera (white part of the eyeball).

consent form   explains a procedure or surgery, including possible risks and complications; patients must sign a consent form before most procedures and all surgeries.

contamination   the unintended contact with unsterile material that may have infectious agents (e.g., bacteria, fungus, virus, and so on).

contraindication   something (as a symptom or condition) that makes a particular treatment or procedure inadvisable.

corticosteroids   a group of synthetic hormones used in the treatment of some leukemias and also to suppress graft rejection and graft-versus-host disease following bone marrow transplant. Side effects include an increased risk of infection.

cortisone cream   a steroid-based cream used topically as an anti-inflammatory.

cosmeceutical   a term used to denote cosmetics that contain an ingredient(s) with some biologic action but which are regulated as cosmetics (e.g., a cosmetic that contains retinol). However, to avoid problems with the FDA, manufacturers list such ingredients as nonactive on the product label.

cosmetic surgery   performed to enhance normal structures of the body to make patients look better or different.

Cosmoderm   an injectable filler bioengineered from human skin.

Cosmoplast   an injectable filler bioengineered from human skin.

Coumadin   a blood thinner; also generically called warfarin.

CRNA   certified registered nurse anesthetist.

crow's feet   the fine skin wrinkles that radiate laterally from around the eyes.

cryosurgery   a surgical procedure that uses freezing temperature from liquid nitrogen or carbon dioxide to destroy tissue. Cryosurgery is used on the skin to remove certain skin lesions (e.g., warts, actinic keratoses, seborrheic keratosis, "age spots," and so on).

cutaneous flap   a flap consisting of skin with some underlying fat.

cyst   A deep fluid-filled cavity.

D

debridement   the process of removing dead (necrotic) devitalized tissue from a wound.

deep venous thrombosis   a blood clot, usually originating in the deep veins of the leg; increased risk after surgery or periods of inactivity.

denaturing   modification of the molecular structure such as a protein with heat, acid, UV light, and so on.

depilatory   an agent used to remove unwanted hair.

dermabrasion   a nonthermal resurfacing procedure that abrades layers of skin through the controlled removal of the epidermis and *upper* dermis. It is performed with an abrasive wheel or brush attached to a high-speed rotary instrument.

dermagraphics   see *permanent cosmetics.*

dermaplaning   the use of the instrument normally used to harvest *split-thickness skin grafts* to shave off damaged skin down into the dermis.

dermatitis   an inflammation of the skin caused by an allergic reaction or contact with an irritant.

dermatology   the medical study and treatment of diseases of the skin, hair, and nails.

dermis   the middle layer of the skin; a complex combination of blood vessels, collagen, elastin, hair follicles, and sebaceous glands.

deviated septum   a condition in which the middle wall (septum) inside the nose deviates into the airway passages; can cause problems breathing through the nose.

diabetes mellitus   a disorder of carbohydrate (sugar) metabolism characterized by inadequate secretions or use of insulin.

diastasis recti   the stretching of the abdominal fascia at the midline, usually as a result of pregnancy.

diplopia   double vision.

dorsal hump   a bump on the nose.

dorsum   term for the back of an anatomic area.

doughnut mastopexy   a single incision procedure done on small ptotic breasts resulting in an inconspicuous circumareolar scar.

dry eye   inadequate lubrication of the eyeball due to exposure or decreased tear production, which can lead to corneal ulceration.

DVT   see *deep venous thrombosis.*

dynamic cooling device   an apparatus attached to a cosmetic laser that emits a short burst of cooling agent milliseconds before each pulse to reduce pain and thermal injury to the surrounding tissue.

dynamic wrinkles   wrinkles in the skin directly above contracting muscles.

dysplastic nevus   an atypical mole that may be a precursor of malignant melanoma.

E

ecchymosis   bruising.

ectropion   the turning out of the edge of the lower eyelid, away from the eyeball.

eczema   a general term for skin inflammation causing redness, dryness, itching, and scaling.

edema   swelling.

EKG   electrocardiogram.

elastin   a protein that works with collagen in the dermis giving structural support to the skin and other organs.

electrocautery   electrical device used to cut the skin or to seal blood vessels to control bleeding during surgery.

electrolysis   process of killing hair follicles with an electric needle.

embolism   blockage of a blood vessel by a small particle that lodges in the lumen (e.g., a blood clot, fat particle, an air bubble, or any of a number of substances).

EMLA cream   a type of topical anesthetic containing lidocaine.

Endermologie   a vacuum, hand-held device, with rollers that "kneads" affected skin areas to reduce cellulite.

endonasal   of or pertaining to inside the nose.

endoscopic surgery   minimal-incision surgery can be performed using tiny cameras and long instruments; typically results in a quicker recovery than surgeries performed with larger incisions.

endotracheal tube   a tube inserted (through the trachea) into the lungs for the purpose of controlled ventilation.

ephelides   freckles.

epinephrine   also known as adrenaline, a medication used to control bleeding and prolong the effect of local anesthetics; works by constricting the blood vessels.

epiphora   watery eyes.

epithelialization   formation of new epidermis over a wound.

erythema   medical term to describe redness of the skin.

erythematous   see *erythema*.

eschars   scabs.

esthetician   one skilled in giving beauty treatments such as facials, manicures, pedicures, and so on. A skin care professional who is devoted to enhancing the health of the skin.

excise   to remove by cutting.

exfoliant   agent that causes the outer layers of skin cells to slough off.

exfoliate   to remove the top layer of skin mechanically or with chemicals.

exophthalmos   a protrusion of one or both eyeballs.

extrinsic aging   changes in the skin due to sun exposure, smoking, and other controllable factors.

exudate   fluid oozing from a healing wound.

eye-lift   see *blepharoplasty*.

F

facial implants   synthetic material employed for augmentation, re-construction, or rejuvenation of the face to enhance facial con-tours, harmony, and balance to the face.

facial veins   see *reticular veins*.

fascia   a thin sheet of fibrous tissue that envelops muscles or groups of muscles. At the far end of muscles, fascia coalesces to become the outermost layers of tendons.

fat embolus   a particle of fat lodged in a blood vessel.

fat grafting   a surgical procedure to remove fat from one area of the body for implanting into another area.

FDA   Food and Drug Administration.

festoon   a pouch of skin and muscle in the lower eyelid and cheek junction.

fibroblasts   the cell that makes collagen.

filler   a substance such as collagen, silicone, or one's own fat that is injected beneath the skin to contour or fill in wrinkles or scars.

fissure   a crack or split in the epidermis.

Fitzpatrick skin types a system to evaluate skin color and assess a person's tendency to tan or burn.

fixation screws used to secure/support tissue (e.g. forehead-lift).

flap a segment of skin, muscle, or bone or any combination of these three components used to close wounds on the body.

follicular unit grafting hair grafts that consist of one to no more than four hairs; these grafts are dissected out under a microscope for greater accuracy.

folliculitis inflammation of hair follicles.

forehead-lift see *brow-lift*.

foreign body something that normally does not belong in body tissues (e.g., piece of glass, splinter, and so on).

free radicals a natural biologic process that results from the body's use of oxygen, chemicals, and even UV radiation.

frontalis muscle the muscle under the skin of the forehead.

FTSG full-thickness skin graft.

full-thickness skin graft consists of epidermis, dermis, and a scant layer of subcutaneous fat used to cover small full-thickness defects, usually on the face.

furuncle a large boil.

G

gastric bypass a surgical procedure to reduce the size of the stomach for the purpose of treating morbid obesity.

gel-filled breast implants breast implants filled with silicone gel.

general anesthesia the administration of certain anesthesia while the patient's airway is controlled by the anesthesiologist or nurse anesthetists; the patient is asleep.

genioplasty a surgical procedure to change the shape of the chin by cutting the bone and changing its position.

gigantomastia large breasts.

gingiva the lining of the gums.

glabella the area between the eyebrows.

glabellar lines vertical forehead creases between the eyebrows.

glutathione the most prevalent antioxidant in the human body.

glycation the cross-linking of sugars to proteins, which inhibits collagen synthesis and creates skin rigidity.

glycolic acid   the AHA most commonly used for *light* chemical peels in the office; popularly known as the "lunch time" peel.

granulation tissue   rounded, fleshy connective tissue projections on the surface of a healing wound; bleeds easily.

Graves' disease   a form of hyperthyroidism.

gynecomastia   enlargement of the male breast.

H

hair restoration surgery   the use of a patient's own hair to restore hair to areas of hair loss (i.e., hair transplants).

hair transplants   see *hair restoration surgery.*

hemangioma   a reddish-purple birthmark consisting of a proliferative vascular tissue; usually raised.

hematoma   a collection of blood outside the blood vessels but still within the confines of tissues or organs of the body; usually completely or partly clotted.

hemoglobin   the oxygen-carrying molecule of red blood cells.

hemophilia   a genetic bleeding disorder in which the blood fails to clot properly.

hemorrhage   heavy bleeding.

hemostasis   control of bleeding.

herpes simplex (I)   causes cold sores and fever blisters.

herpes simplex (II)   causes genital lesions; sexually transmitted.

hirsutism   a condition characterized by excess facial hair.

histologic   of or pertaining to cells.

histology   the microscopic study of cells.

hormone   a chemical substance produced by different glands that travels through the bloodstream to influence other tissues and glands.

HTN   hypertension.

hydroquinone   a bleaching agent to lighten the skin.

hyperesthesia   a condition of having abnormally sensitive skin, which can occur after bruising or injury to a nerve.

hyperhidrosis   profuse sweating.

hyperpigmentation   a skin condition in which there is excessive pigmentation.

hyperplasia   an increase in the number of cells.

hypertension   high blood pressure.

hypertonic saline   high concentration of sodium.

hypertrophic scar   a raised, red scar that, unlike a keloid scar, stays within the boundaries of the wound.

hypoallergenic   a product designed to reduce the chance of allergic reaction.

hypopigmentation   a skin condition in which there is a diminished pigmentation.

hypoxia   extremely low levels of oxygen.

I

immunosuppressants   anything that suppresses the immune system.

indication   symptom, condition, or particular circumstance that indicates the advisability or necessity of a specific medical treatment or procedure.

inferior   anatomic term referring to a position below an area or body part.

inflammation   redness, swelling, and pain as a result of irritation, injury, or infection.

inflammatory cells   white blood cells.

inframammary   underneath the breast. Indicates the location of one of the possible incisions for breast enlargement.

inframammary fold   of or relating to the area below the breasts.

infra-orbital rim   the rim of bone that comprises the lower eye socket.

injectable fillers   collagen, autologous fat or other suitable substances employed to plump up wrinkles and facial creases, furrows, "sunken" cheeks, skin depressions, and some types of scars. They can also add fullness to the lips and cheeks.

injection liposculpture   see *mesotherapy*.

inpatient   a person receiving medical or surgical treatment who requires a short- or long-term hospital stay.

intima   the lining of a blood vessel.

intravenous   through the vein.

intravenous sedation   calming medication administered directly through a vein.

intrinsic aging   changes due to the passage of time and genetics.

intubation insertion of a tube in the trachea for the purpose of ventilation.

ischemia inadequate delivery of oxygen and other nutrients due to lack of blood flow to the tissue.

IV intravenous.

J

Jessner's solution a face peel solution consisting of salicylic acid, resorcinol, and lactic acid.

jowls the fleshy part of the cheek that (with aging) begins to hang below the lower edge of the jaw; from the cheek to the angle of the mandible.

K

keloid scar a type of scar that continues to grow, and grow, and grow beyond what is needed at the site of an injury due to too much collagen deposition.

keratin a protein substance that forms the outer layer of skin, hair, and nails.

keratinocyte an epidermal cell that produces keratin.

keratosis any lesion on the epidermis marked by the presence of circumscribed overgrowths of the horny layer.

L

labial of or pertaining to the lips.

lactic acid a popular AHA found in many over-the-counter cosmetic products as well as prescription moisturizers.

lagophthalmos the inability to close the upper eyelid completely.

laryngeal mask anesthesia a small plastic device that covers the larynx directly to deliver anesthetic and oxygen to a patient under general anesthesia.

laser skin resurfacing the use of lasers to improve the appearance of the skin.

lateral anatomic location, meaning to the side.

lichenification thickening of the epidermis with underlying inflammation, giving the skin a "morocco leather" appearance with exaggeration of normal skin lines.

lidocaine   a commonly used local anesthetic.

ligation   to tie off, as in tying off a varicose vein.

light chemical face peel   the acids in this group are mild, allowing the gentle exfoliation of the epidermis. This level of peel will usually not effect the dermis.

lip reduction   to reduce the size of the lips by incisions within the mouth.

lipodystrophy   disturbance of fat metabolism (e.g., love handles, double chin, and so on).

lipolysis   the breakdown of fat.

lipoma   a benign fatty tumor.

lipoplasty   same as liposuction.

liposculpture   same as liposuction.

liposuction   the removal of body fat through small skin incisions, using a cannula and aspirator.

liquid nitrogen   dry ice used to exfoliate some abnormal skin lesions by freezing.

LMA   see *laryngeal mask anesthesia*.

local anesthesia   injecting an anesthetic directly in the area where a procedure is being performed for the purpose of eliminating pain during the procedure.

lunch time peel   see *light chemical face peel*.

lupus   a connective tissue disorder, sometimes diagnosed by a butterfly-shaped, red rash on the face.

lymph fluid   a clear fluid that resembles blood plasma, containing primarily white blood cells.

lymphangitis   superficial (skin) red streaking extending from areas of infection toward the regional lymph nodes. This is due to inflamed lymphatic vessels, requiring immediate medical attention.

lymphedema   regional swelling resulting from obstruction of lymphatic vessels.

M

macrogenia   a large chin.

macromastia   large breasts.

macule   a flat spot or patch of a different color from the surrounding skin (e.g., freckles).

malar of or pertaining to cheekbone(s).

malignant of or pertaining to cancer.

mammaplasty any reconstructive or cosmetic surgical procedure that alters the size or shape of the breast.

mammography special breast X-ray used to detect breast cancer.

marionette lines the lines of aging or skin folds on either side of the chin, just anterior to the jowls.

mastectomy a surgical procedure in which all or part of the breast is removed; usually secondary to cancer.

mastitis inflammation of the breast; usually due to an infection.

mastopexy see *breast-lift*.

mechanism of action how something works or achieves its goal(s).

medial term meaning of or toward the anatomic (vertical) midline.

medical spa a facility that operates under the full-time, on-site supervision of a licensed healthcare professional. The facility operates within the scope of practice of its staff and offers traditional, complementary, and alternative health practices and treatments in a spa-like setting.

medispa see *medical spa*.

melanin a pigment in the skin or hair that gives it its tan or dark color.

melanocyte a cell that produces melanin.

melanoma the most dangerous form of skin cancer; the most likely skin cancer to metastasize.

melasma a condition in which pigmentation of the cheeks of the face darkens into tan or brown patches; often occurs during pregnancy.

mentoplasty same as chin augmentation.

mesotherapy the microinjection of minute amounts of concentrated agents (conventional and/or homeopathic medications, plant extracts, vitamins, and nutrients) into the skin at various depths and amounts for body contouring.

metastasize the spread of the primary cancer to other areas of the body.

microdermabrasion uses a hand-held device that forcibly propels a stream of tiny, sterile crystals onto the skin surface, resulting in gentle abrasion that stimulates the production of new skin cells and collagen, which gives the skin a fresh, healthy glow.

microgenia   small chin.

micrognathia   small mandible.

micrografts   hair grafts that contain one or two hairs per graft unit.

micropigmentation   see *permanent cosmetics*.

microtia   small ear(s).

minigrafts   hair grafts that contain three or six hairs per graft unit.

Mohs chemo surgery   piecemeal excision of a skin lesion with immediate microscopic exam to ensure a safe margin of excision.

mole   a benign skin growth that is usually pigmented; also called a nevus.

motor nerve   a nerve that causes muscular movement.

MRI   magnetic resonance imaging.

Myobloc   a form of *botulinum toxin*.

N

nasal dorsum   the bridge of the nose.

nasal turbinates   areas of bone and mucosa projecting from the lateral walls of the nasal cavity that warms and humidifies inhaled air; can sometimes cause nasal airway obstruction.

nasolabial folds   the line extending from the nostrils to the corner of the mouth.

NCEA   National Coalition of Esthetic and Related Associations.

neck lift   surgery to remove excess neck skin.

necrosis   cellular/tissue death.

necrotic tissue   nonviable or dead tissue.

nerve block   injection of local anesthetic next to a nerve to numb the area that it innervates.

nevi   pleural for nevus.

nevus   a benign growth on the skin that is usually pigmented; also called a mole.

nipple-sharing techniques   using part of one nipple to reconstruct the contralateral nipple in breast reconstruction.

nodule   usually indicates small, firm, raised, lump deeply set in the skin.

nonablative lasers   lasers that do not disturb the superficial layer of the skin.

nose job see *rhinoplasty*.

NPO nothing by mouth.

NSAID nonsteroidal anti-inflammatory drugs (e.g., Motrin).

nurse anesthetist a nurse trained and specializing in the administration of anesthesia.

nutraceuticals nutritional supplements; including antioxidants. Although this spelling has made it into print media, the correct spelling is nutriceutical because it refers to nutrition, which contains the letter "i".

nutriceuticals nutritional supplements; including antioxidants.

O

occlusive mask a nonpermeable tape applied immediately after certain face peels to increase the penetration of the peel, increasing its efficacy.

Occupational Safety and Health Administration a branch of the U.S. Department of Labor that assures the safety and health of America's workers by setting and enforcing standards; providing training, outreach, and education; establishing partnerships; and encouraging continual improvement in workplace safety and health.

ocular of or pertaining to the eyes.

off-label use the legal use of a drug for an indication other than that for which it was approved for by the FDA.

oncogenes a gene having the potential to cause a normal cell to become cancerous.

onychomycosis A fungal infection of the nails causing discoloration, thickening, and splitting of the nails.

open rhinoplasty surgery of the nose involving an incision across the columella between the nostrils, which can leave a faint scar.

orbicularis oculi muscle a circular muscle sheet that surrounds the external area of the orbit of the eye.

orbicularis oris muscle a circular muscle sheet that surrounds the lips.

orbital of or pertaining to the eye socket.

OSHA see *Occupational Safety and Health Administration*.

otoplasty the pinning back of prominent ears.

outpatient a person receiving medical or surgical treatment who does not need to stay overnight at the medical facility.

P

palate   the roof of the mouth.

palpebral   of or pertaining to the eyelid.

palsy   a partial or total paralysis (e.g., Bell's palsy).

panniculectomy   surgical excision of redundant, apron-like, over-hanging lower abdominal tissue. Particularly after massive weight loss.

papillary dermis   the upper layer of the dermis.

papules   small raised lesions on the skin; usually red.

paralysis   loss of motor function; inability to *actively* move a muscle.

paronychia   infection of the cuticle of the finger.

pectoralis muscle   the major muscle of the chest or "the pecs."

pendulous breasts   large hanging breasts.

Penrose drain   surgical drain made of thin plastic.

periareolar   of or pertaining to the region around the areola.

perioral   of or pertaining to the region around the mouth.

periorbital   of or pertaining to the region around the eye socket.

periorbital fat   fat supporting the upper and lower eyelids.

periosteum   a thin layer of firm tissue covering bones.

permanent cosmetics   pigment is injected directly into the reticular dermis via fine needles resulting in permanent tattooing; used for creating a permanent lip color, eyeliner, and even tattooing a permanent areola after breast reconstruction.

permanent makeup   see *permanent cosmetics.*

phenol   a chemical used for deep face peels.

phlebitis   inflammation of a vein.

photo-aging   wrinkles and age spots that occur to the skin due to history of overexposure to the sun's UV light.

photophobia   excessive tearing due to light sensitivity.

photosensitivity   an abnormal sensitivity to light, increasing the chances of severe sunburn; often caused by medication.

photothermolysis   destruction of tissue using heat created by a high-energy light source (e.g., laser resurfacing).

physician assistant   a person licensed to practice medicine under the supervision of a licensed physician.

pilosebaceous unit   hair follicle with its contributing sebaceous gland.

pineal gland   a small appendage of the brain.

pityriasis versicolor   same as tinea versicolor.

plaque   a raised uniform thickening of a portion of the skin with a well-defined edge and a flat or rough surface (e.g., psoriasis).

platysma muscle   the superficial muscle sheet of the neck that extends from the clavicles to the jaw.

platysmal bands   the visible, midline, vertical edges of the platysma muscle.

platysmaplasty   surgical repair of the lax medial margins of the platysma muscle in the *submental* area.

port-wine stain   a flat, congenital overabundance of blood vessels beneath the surface of the skin.

posterior   anatomic location, meaning behind.

PRN   medical short-hand meaning as needed.

prone position   lying face down.

prophylactic   preventative measure, as in antibiotics taken before and/or after surgery to prevent infection.

pruritus   itching.

pseudofolliculitis   ingrown hairs usually on the face/neck that cause redness, bumps, and sometimes pus.

psoriasis   a chronic skin condition where the skin cells multiply at a very rapid rate, creating a silver whitish scale that itches; can be painful. Most common on the hands, scalp, and knees.

PT   lab test to determine blood clotting.

ptosis   the drooping of a body part, especially the eyelids or the breasts.

PTT   lab test to determine blood clotting.

pulmonary   of or pertaining to the lungs.

pulmonary embolism   an obstruction in the pulmonary artery due to a clot; most commonly, a blood clot; impairs breathing and can be lethal.

purified botulinum toxin   a toxin derived from *Clostridium botulinum* used in *aesthetic medicine* to treat dynamic wrinkles.

pustule   a skin bleb filled with pus.

physiology   the science concerned with the normal vital processes of organisms.

Q

QD   medical short-hand for "once every day."

QOD   medical short-hand for "once every other day."

R

RBC   red blood cells.

reconstructive surgery   performed to correct or repair abnormal structures of the body caused by congenital defects, developmental abnormalities, trauma, infection, tumors, or disease so as to improve function or create a normal appearance to the extent possible.

reduction mammaplasty   see *breast reduction*.

reepithelialized   when epithelial cells once again cover the wound.

resorcinol   a chemical peeling agent; also used in the treatment of acne and pigmentary disorders; an ingredient in Jessner's solution.

reticular dermis   the lower layer of the dermis.

rhinophyma   a condition characterized by gradually enlarging, redness, and misshapen nose with enlarged pores; it is the result of skin and sebaceous gland overgrowth and proliferation of blood vessels; associated with rosacea and alcoholism.

rhinoplasty   the nasal architecture is surgically altered to attain the desired size and shape.

rhytidectomy   face-lift.

rhytids   wrinkles.

rosacea   an acneiform condition characterized by facial redness, flushing, papules, and pustules with the formation of prominent blood vessels in the face.

S

SAL   see *suction-assisted liposuction*.

salicylic acid   see *beta hydroxy acid*.

saline   sterile, slightly salted water.

saline-filled breast implants   breast implants filled with saline.

scales   flakes or flat horny cells loosened from the stratum corneum (horny layer).

scalpel   a surgical blade/knife.

scalp flap   a peninsula of the hair-bearing scalp used to repair an adjacent scalp defect or bald area. It remains "tethered" to its original blood supply for uninterrupted circulation.

scalp reduction   to reduce or completely eliminate a bald area of the crown and/or mid-scalp; the bald scalp is excised, then the adjacent hair-bearing scalp tissue is stretched and the resulting scalp margins are sutured together.

scar contracture   a permanent tightening of skin that occurs; often in response to a burn.

scleroderma   a connective tissue disorder causing hardening of the skin and other organs.

sclerosing solution   a solution that when injected into the lumen of a small vein causes injury to the lining with resulting obliteration of that vein(s).

sclerotherapy   the obliteration of certain veins by injecting a *sclerosing solution* directly into the lumen of the vein, causing the vein to disappear within a short period of time.

scurvy   a condition resulting from vitamin C deficiency characterized by problems associated with poorly formed collagen and the resulting effect on body tissues, including poor healing with low tensile strength of wounds and so on.

sebaceous glands   oil-producing glands of the skin that emit oil into and through the hair follicles.

seborrheic dermatitis   commonly known as dandruff. Can also occur on ears, axilla, and pubic area. Characterized by redness and scaling appearance in varying degrees. The scales may be dry or greasy.

seborrheic keratosis   elevated, light tan to dark brown (1–3 cm), greasy, wart-like growths that characteristically appear "stuck on" to the surface of the skin; common among the elderly.

sebum   oil from sebaceous glands.

sedation   the act of calming a patient with a sedative during a procedure; the patient is awake but in no discomfort.

sedative   an agent that quiets nervous excitement.

senile lentigo   age spots.

sensory nerve   peripheral nerves that detect, touch, pain, temperature, and so on.

septoplasty   a surgical procedure to improve the flow of air through the nose by repairing deviated septal cartilage.

seroma   a collection of serum within the confines of postsurgical tissues or organs of the body.

serum   the clear liquid that separates from blood.

shave biopsy   the harvesting of a raised skin lesion for microscopic evaluation (biopsy). It is shaved off at the level of the skin. This should not be done when there is a high index of suspicion that the lesion might be a melanoma, because the depth of the lesion is critical for staging and prognosis.

silicone sheeting   a silicone dressing placed over a raised scar to soften and flatten it.

skin grafts   skin harvested from one area to cover a defect in a different area. See "split-thickness" skin grafts and "full-thickness" skin grafts.

skin resurfacing   the improvement of the facial skin with chemical, laser, or mechanical abrasion.

skin tag   tiny benign, fleshy growth commonly found on the neck, under the arms, and on the eyelid.

sloughing   dead cells falling off of living cells (e.g., skin cells) to separate from living tissue.

SMAS   see *superficial musculoaponeurotic system.*

smoker's lip lines   the lines/wrinkles that radiate from the lips of people who have smoked cigarettes for many years; more prominent in the upper lips.

SOB   shortness of breath.

SPCP   Society of Permanent Cosmetic Professionals.

SPF   see *sun protection factor.*

split-thickness skin graft   a thin sheet of epidermis together with some dermis that is harvested; usually from the thigh. The donor area is reepithelialized from the epidermis lining the pilosebaceous units.

squamous cell   A keratin-producing cell of the epidermis.

squamous cell carcinoma   a malignant form of skin cancer. Usually worse than *basal cell* skin cancer but not as bad as *melanoma.*

stat   to be done now, immediately, urgently.

steroids   a large family of chemical substances, comprising many hormones, vitamins, and drugs.

steri-strips   small adhesive strip commonly used on sutured wounds and after the sutures are removed.

stratum corneum   the outer most layer of the epidermis.

stretch marks   commonly found on the abdomen after pregnancy and weight gain.

striae distensae   stretch marks.

STSG   split-thickness skin graft.

subcutaneous   of or pertaining to the area immediately below the skin.

subcuticular   of or pertaining to the area below the epidermis.

submental   the anatomic area within the area of the triangular margins of the mandible; where the double chin resides.

submuscular   of or pertaining to a position below a muscle.

subpectoral   of or relating to below the pectoralis muscle, as in placement of a breast implant.

subperiosteal   of or pertaining to an area under the periosteum.

sub Q   of or relating to below the skin.

suction-assisted liposuction   see *liposuction*

sun protection factor   represents the ability of an agent to delay sun-induced redness of the skin.

superficial   pertaining to or situated near the surface.

superficial face peel   see *light peel.*

superficial musculoaponeurotic system   a layer of tissue that covers the deeper structures in the cheek area and is in continuity with the superficial muscle covering the lower face and neck, called the platysma. Some face-lift techniques lift and reposition the SMAS as well as the skin.

superior   anatomic term referring to a position above an area or body part.

supine   lying face up.

sutures   the stitches used to hold tissue together or to close a wound.

synthetic of or relating to being produced by chemical synthesis.

systemic relating to entire organism rather than its individual parts.

T

TCA see *trichloroacetic acid.*

telangiectasias tiny red-blue vascular lesion created by the abnormal dilatation of preexisting small veins.

temporal scalp the scalp just above the ears and behind the forehead.

tensile strength the largest stress that tissue can bear without tearing apart.

thread lift a minimally invasive face-lift using special subcutaneous *suspension sutures* for subtle changes.

thrombophlebitis a blood clot with local pain and tenderness.

thrombosis intravascular or intracardiac clotting.

thrombus a blood clot.

thymol iodine powder a solution used after a face peel to create a heavy crust.

TID short-hand for "three times per day."

tinea a general term for fungal infections of the hair, nails, and skin.

tinea capitis ringworm of the scalp.

tinea corporis ringworm.

tinea cruris "jock" itch.

tinea pedis athlete's foot.

tinea versicolor a yeast infection of the skin; precipitated by heat.

tissue expander a plastic or silicone container placed subcutaneously for expansion of the overlying skin/scalp through an injection port.

tragus the small projection of cartilage in front of the opening of the ear canal.

TRAM flap see *transverse rectus abdominis myocutaneous.*

transconjunctival an internal incision used in a lower blepharoplasty.

transumbilical breast augmentation the insertion of a breast implant via an incision through the umbilicus.

transverse rectus abdominis myocutaneous flap   a myocutaneous flap taken from the lower abdomen. It consists of muscle, fat, and skin from the abdomen; commonly used in postmastectomy breast re-construction.

trichloroacetic acid   a solution commonly used for medium and deep face peels.

TUBA   see *transumbilical breast augmentation.*

tumescent liposuction   this technique involves injecting a large volume of solution into the area(s) to be treated prior to suctioning—as much as three times the amount of fat to be removed.

tummy tuck   see *abdominoplasty.*

tumor   an abnormal mass of tissue. Tumors can be benign or malignant (cancerous).

turbinates   see *nasal turbinates.*

turbinectomy   surgical excision of the turbinates to improve nasal airflow.

turkey neck   slang for redundant *submental* skin and fat and/or prominent medial margins of the *platysma* muscle.

U

UAL   see *ultrasound assisted liposuction.*

ulcer   an area of total loss of skin or mucous membrane.

ultrasound-assisted liposuction   using an ultrasound instrument in liposuction.

ultraviolet light   a specific range of wavelength of sunlight that damages skin and causes skin cancer.

umbilicus   belly button; navel.

UV   see *ultraviolet.*

UVA   ultraviolet light that causes aging and damage to elastin and collagen in the skin as well as tanning.

UVB   ultraviolet light that causes reddening and some tanning of the skin.

V

varicose veins   dilated, enlarged (>0.25 inches) and tortuous veins, usually on the legs.

vascular   of or pertaining to the blood vessels.

vasoconstriction   the constriction, or narrowing, of a blood vessel.

vasodilatation   the dilatation of a blood vessel.

vein stripping   the surgical removal of varicose veins through two tiny incisions.

vermillion border   the edge of the red pigment around the lips.

vesicle   a tiny blister (e.g., herpes simplex).

viscosity   flow properties of fluid.

vitiligo   irregular areas of depigmented skin. Most commonly these depigmented areas occur on the face and the dorsum of the hands and feet, but they can occur anywhere on the skin.

W

warfarin   a blood thinner. Also called Coumadin.

warm compress   a warm pad or gauze applied to certain wounds.

wart   a benign lump on the skin caused by the human papilloma virus.

WBC   white blood cells.

white line   the outer edge of the lips where fillers are placed to accentuate lip fullness.

X

xanthelasma   round or oval, slightly elevated yellowish lesions located on the eyelids that consist of fat deposits that have been deposited between the skin and underlying eyelid muscle.

Z

Zyderm   an injectable filler purified from bovine (cow) collagen.

Zyplast   an injectable filler purified from bovine (cow) collagen.

Index

Note: Page entries marked
t are tables; entries marked
f are figures

Notes